# CROSSCURRENTS
PURSUING SOCIAL JUSTICE AND INTERRELIGIOUS WORK
SINCE 1950

*CrossCurrents* (ISSN 0011-1953; online ISSN 1939-3881) connects the wisdom of the heart with the life of the mind and the experiences of the body. The journal is operated through its parent organization, the Association for Public Religion and Intellectual Life (APRIL), an interreligious network of academics, activists, artists, and community leaders seeking to engage the many ways religion meets the public. Contributions to the journal exist at the nexus of religion, education, the arts, and social justice. The journal is published quarterly on behalf of the Association for Public Religion and Intellectual Life by the University of North Carolina Press.

The Association for Public Religion and Intellectual Life (formerly ARIL) is a global network of leaders, scholars, and social change agents who explore religious life, engage in intellectual inquiry, and lead ethical action in the world today. Their primary objective, especially through annual summer colloquia and *CrossCurrents*, is to bring together leading voices of our time to advocate for justice and to examine global spiritual and interreligious currents in both historical and contemporary perspectives.

A membership to APRIL includes access to *CrossCurrents* starting with Volume 58, 2008, though our partners at Project MUSE, monthly newsletters, early access to summer colloquium themes, a 40% on UNC Press books, and more. For more information, including membership and subscription rates, visit www.aprilonline.org.

This reissue of *CrossCurrents* was one of four issues published in 2017 as part of Volume 67. For a current masthead visit www.aprilonline.org.

© 2017 Association for Public Religion and Intellectual Life. All rights reserved.

ISBN 978-1-4696-6689-1 (Print)

# CROSSCURRENTS

VOLUME 67, NO 4  ISSN 0011-1953

## AMBIGUITY

**653**
*Ambiguity*
**Anne Foerst**

**666**
*About the Cover Art*
**Tobi Kahn**

**668**
*Japanese American Spiritual Ambiguity and Arts of Silence*
**Brett J. Esaki**

**681**
*Belief and Delusion as Palliative Responses to Uncertainty*
**Philip R. Corlett**

**696**
*"Clear as God's Words"?–Dealing with Ambiguities in the Bible*
**Manfred Oeming**

**705**
*More Choice, Less Uncertainty: The Paradoxical Relationship of Political Identity and News Exposure in the American Public Sphere*
**Benjamin Gross**

**726**
*Why the Wende?*
**Peter Heinegg**

**730**
*The Road to Monotheism*
**Peter Heinegg**

**734**
*Do They Contradict Themselves?*
*Very Well Then They Contradict Themselves*
**Peter Heinegg**

**744**
*Notes on Contributors*

# CROSSCURRENTS
## AMBIGUITY

Anne Foerst

Ambiguity is imbedded in the texture of our life. Most complex phenomena, most of our urgent questions and ultimate concerns, and most of our sensory perceptions are inherently ambiguous. And like all terms that describe complex phenomena, the term "ambiguous" is ambiguous (pun intended...). On the one hand, ambiguity implies uncertainty and the lack of clarity. On the other hand, we use the term "ambiguity" to describe phenomena with multiple meanings or interpretations.

Both meanings of the term are closely related. When we are confronted with uncertainty, we seek certainty. This means, any ambiguous phenomenon in the first sense of the word is asking for a more in-depth understanding that overcomes uncertainty. However, we are using the same strategy for ambiguity in the second sense of the word. We are deeply uncomfortable with multiple meanings and are, therefore, often inclined to declare one meaning correct and the other irrelevant or even incorrect. It is intrinsically human to avoid ambiguity and to reduce complex phenomena into simpler theories that can be easily understood.

Ambiguity has often been analyzed in the context of language. Early attempts at machine language led to a slew of analyses on the ambiguity of language in order to enable machine to understand and re-create natural language. In today's technical environments where Siri, Alexa, and other language-based avatars are ubiquitous, such analyses seem to be obsolete. However, everyone who ever worked with such avatars or even simple language-based search engines knows how often these systems misunderstand.

It is naïve to assume that every word means always the same and, yet, this is an assumption that many of us subconsciously hold. However, "Ambiguity is not a rare freak; it permeates language as much as water permeates an organism."[1] According to Robinson, there are several levels of ambiguity in language. The first and most simple is the ambiguity found in words such as "this" and "she" which have different meanings nearly every time they are used; however, their meaning can be easily determined based on context. Proper nouns are also inherently ambiguous but can easily be clarified and understood.

A more complex form of ambiguity can be found in terms that describe a large complex of conceptions that are somehow felt to belong together. Robinson brings up the example of *virtue* that can have meanings on a whole scale of conceptions. Making money can be seen as virtue as well as giving all money away to the poor. Here, the ambiguity of the term lies in the scale on which the specific meaning, depending on the context, can slide up or down.

Then there are numerous examples of words having completely unconnected meanings. "Time flies like and arrow and fruit flies like a banana" is among the better-known examples. Again, context can help to clarify; but such double meanings are also a wonderful source for puns and humor.

Context is the way to solve most language ambiguities. Not only can the context make the meaning of an ambiguous phrase clear, we also create context when the ambiguity is too strong, and even construct meaning out of gibberish. For instance, when talking to a friend in a noisy bar, we will believe we understand her perfectly even though we might miss most of her words, because we will fill the gaps of her speech based on our knowledge of her and the topics discussed.

A beautiful example of creating language patterns out of gibberish can be found in Edgar Allen Poe's *The Murders in the Rue Morgue* where all witnesses who have heard the "conversation" between the sailor and his Orangutan are sure that the dialogue partner of the sailor spoke a foreign language. They all clearly recognize a specific language even though they all recognize a language they themselves do not speak...

This means there are two strategies coping with language ambiguity. We either detect patterns of meaning out of contextual cues, or we create patterns of meaning.

The most complex form of ambiguity in language can be found when a word can have different, somewhat connected meanings. In dialogue, people using the same word might attach very different meanings or connotations to it. For example, a computer scientist will use the term "information" very differently from a librarian. Meanings of terms can differ due to different backgrounds, geographies, and worldviews. In dialogue, such ambiguities can create misunderstandings which are very difficult to resolve because people are usually not aware that they use terms differently. When they listen to their dialogue partner, they are sure to understand what he or she is saying even if they might have meant something altogether different with the same terminology.

Robinson sees the reason for such misunderstandings in the complexity of certain phenomena whose meaning language can only approximate but not fully describe.

> There is no genus identical in healthy exercise and healthy complexion and healthy roses. The word is used to indicate now this and now that relation to health. Exercise causes health; complexion indicates health; roses possess health. What particular relation to health is meant in each particular case has to be learned from the context.[2]

Again, context is key but the full meaning of a term can still elude us. While in Robinson's example, all three meanings refer to the concept of health, we still cannot unambiguously define the term "health."

This means, the most complex form of ambiguity in language is rooted in another form of ambiguity: the ambiguity of reality. Robinson himself explains the ambiguities of our perceived reality with our incomplete knowledge of the world. The underlying assumption here is that ambiguity as such is not real but, rather, the result of incomplete knowledge or recognition. This, however, brings us back to our initial definition. Is ambiguity a phenomenon that is real and cannot be resolved or is ambiguity the result of incomplete knowledge? We won't be able to solve this epistemological debate in this forum. But we will approach the concept of ambiguity through shared experiences and their analyses.

AMBIGUITY

Let's look at one famous example for ambiguity, the face–vase picture.

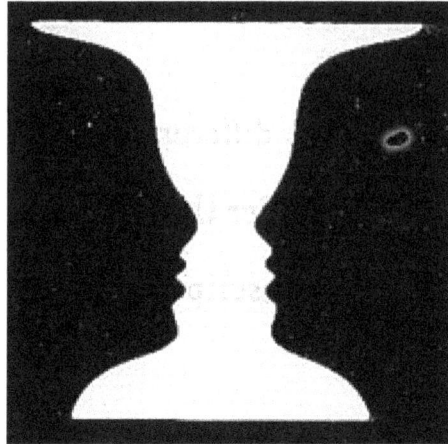

In this picture, we can either see two faces (in black) or a vase (in white). When we concentrate on the vase, the faces can still be seen but they become less prominent. When we concentrate on the faces, the vase moves into the background. However, at no moment will we be able to see both the vase and the faces simultaneously and with equal clarity. If we concentrate on seeing both, we will start oscillating between the two images and see a very quick change from faces to vase to faces and back.

Just from this simple interaction with a well-known image, we can learn a very important aspect of ambiguity. Humans do not just have psychological problems to recognize it as such but our brain doesn't support its perception either.

When confronted with a sensory input with multiple meanings, we quickly make a decision for one meaning and perceive only that. And the meaning we most likely perceive depends on the context. Our experiences and expectations will shape our perceptions. We subconsciously assume that what we perceive is a perfect image of the outside world. However, we do not perceive what's out there—whatever that might be—but, rather, what we expect to see. Our brain forms expectations that will guide our senses.

In the face–vase picture, we will most likely see whatever fits the context. If the image were to be among different pictures of vases, we most likely would focus on the vase and might not even see the two faces. On the other hand, if the image were placed with other depictions of faces, we most likely would see just the faces and not the vase.

Social interactions add another dimension to our dealings with ambiguity. If a majority of our community were to opt for one meaning, we most likely would agree with them—in fact, our very perceptions would lead us to agree. Again, our perception apparatus does not sense an objective world. Rather, we will sense what we expect to sense. Expectations, prejudices, and preconceived notions will shape all of our observations. So, when being part of a group, our perceptions will support what the expectations of the group are. Imagine a group standing in front of the face–vase picture agreeing—based on worldviews, expectations, context, etc.—that it depicts two faces. Most members of this group cannot even imagine that another group might see a vase in this image.

There are numerous experiments that provide solid data on how humans cope with ambiguity. When confronted with choices, we prefer making these choices in a context where we have some knowledge of the probabilities of the expected outcomes. For instance, when given the choice of betting on blue vs red ball chosen from either a box with 50% of each vs a random number of each, most of us will choose the box with equal distribution even though our chances might increase otherwise because the distribution might be 80/20 in our favor. In other words, when given the choice between a random but likely favorable outcome and an outcome that has a clearly defined probability, humans tend to choose the calculable probability rather than the uncertain one. These findings have a strong impact on economics and marketing. When confronted with several seemingly comparative buying options, consumers tend to prefer establish brands rather than take a risk. And they will do so believing that their choice is well-informed.[3]

Ambiguity aversion is a well-established phenomenon in economics and behavioral studies. It can be found in competitive markets and can impact asset prices and portfolio choices—a finding that stumped the economics world when first published.[4] Stock values are not determined by what a company is actually worth but by the faith stock traders put into their potential. And ambiguity avoidance makes us often opt for potentials that our society agrees upon. The reason for the tech bubble that burst quite spectacularly in 2001 was that everyone put high expectations into technology—and since this was the majority opinion, buying tech stocks, not matter what the inflated price, seemed less ambiguous than buying other stock.

Also from the world of economics comes the *comparative ignorance hypothesis* that suggests that people "are more willing to bet on their vague beliefs in situations in which they feel particularly knowledgeable."[5] The operative word here is "feel" because the competence in such a situation does not need to be measurable or truly present but only strongly be felt. Only if people don't feel particularly competent, do they prefer to bet on clear probabilities. The belief in one's own competence will lead to decision making that seems unambiguous. This can also mean that we create the belief in our own competency to avoid ambiguous decision making; we avoid doubt in our own competency to cater to our instinct of ambiguity avoidance.

The Bible is well aware of the human unwillingness and incapability to deal with ambiguities and calls it "sin." The term "sin" addresses our estrangement from God, from others, and from ourselves. This estrangement is caused by our partial knowledge and our desire toward coherency. Even if "sin" in everyday language is used for supposedly bad acts, in contemporary theology "sin" is usually translated with "estrangement."

This understanding of sin has its—metaphorical—origin in what is usually called "the Fall" (Gen 2-4). Traditionally, the story is told as follows: Adam and Eve live in the Garden happily, in unity with God and all other creatures. They can go wherever they want to go; they can eat and drink whatever they want. In the whole garden, there are only two trees they are not allowed to eat from, The Tree of Knowledge of Good and Evil and the Tree of Life. One day, Eve is tempted by a serpent to eat from the Tree of Knowledge (as it is usually called) and thus acts against God's explicit wish. She also convinces Adam to have a bite and therefore they have to leave paradise. The "sin" here is disobedience against God's command.

But is this really the only way to read this story? Paul Tillich[6] suggests another interpretation that might have more explanatory power—especially in the context of our incapability to deal with ambiguities. As Tillich points out, in the Garden of Eden there was no ambiguity. Everything was in perfect unity and harmony. According to the Biblical narrative, the ability to distinguish between good and evil and to make universally valid judgments is God's and God's alone. Human knowledge is always partial and incomplete; therefore, we cannot achieve the full divine understanding that would explain unexplainable phenomena and would make the world coherent. We do not have divine knowledge and therefore we are not capable of judging; we are not allowed to eat from The Tree of Knowledge of Good and Evil.

But the humans in Paradise also had no will. They didn't make decisions. They did not think, compare, categorize. When they ate from the forbidden fruit, it was the fruit of The Tree of *Knowledge of Good and Evil*. Before this, they did not know what was good and what was evil. They did not decide what was right or wrong. They just were. But with the fruits of the forbidden tree came the human capability to err and to make mistakes.

But if humans do not make decisions and judge and use reason, they do not use what is potentially given to them. Humans who do not try to understand themselves and the world around them, humans who do not try to make judgments, are in a state of what Tillich calls *dreaming innocence*. To actualize our potential, we have to try to become like God (in the language of the story: to eat from the tree) and thus risk the close relationship with God. Since humans are in most ways like other animals, they are limited in time and space. This makes every judgment incomplete. With eating from the tree, humans risk error, incomplete knowledge, and false judgments.

The very first insight that comes with judgment is the perception of the other as other. The category of "otherness" is a fundamental category that humans learn to recognize between thirty-six and forty months of age. A famous test for the development of the category of otherness is the "Sally and Anne" experiment.[7] Children are shown two girls, Anne and Sally. While Anne has a basket in front of her, Sally has a box. Now, Anne will put a ball into her basket and leave the room. Sally, then, takes the ball out of Anne's basket and puts it in her box instead. The children are now asked where Anne, when she comes back, will search for her ball. Their answers are measured by how long they watch either the basket or the box.

Children pass this test easily when they are at least thirty-six months old. Before this age however, they cannot conceptualize that Anne, who was not present when Sally switched the ball, will of course look in her own basket. They have no concept of other people being really other people with different perspectives and outlooks. Only when they are at least three years old, do they have the insight that people who did not see a specific action will not act according to it. Now, they realize that Anne was not present and know that she will look in her own box.

Our sense of self develops only when there is a sense of the other as the other. Only when I realize that there are other people with different perspectives, will I learn to distinguish between them and me. Self-awareness is not something inherent in every human but is learned and developed in social interaction between the child and the people around her.

The judgment of the other as different from self is, however, not the first of our experiences of otherness. Studies have shown that six months old babies have no difficulties to distinguish between different chimp faces.[8] Now, we usually think that most chimps look pretty much alike and so it is amazing that children so small can distinguish them. However, with six months of age, children become experts in distinguishing faces they are surrounded with and lose the capability to distinguish between faces in general.

One explanation for this finding is that when babies are born, they are at the very beginning of the events of bonding that will start to develop at the moment of birth. All inbuilt social mechanisms are active but they are purely instinctive and reactive, without inner connection. The facial recognition apparatus is one of them and helps babies to distinguish faces from non-faces. Over time, every child becomes a specialist for the faces she is surrounded with and cannot anymore distinguish between faces that are principally different, being it the faces of chimps or sheep or, unfortunately, faces of human beings she is not surrounded with.

Infants also react to any sound. However, with about six months of age they react more strongly to sounds from the language they are surrounded with and react negatively to unfamiliar sounds.[9]

However, the relationship between self and other is ambiguous. The other can be a parent, friend, and partner; someone needed for survival and love. But the other can also be a foe, dangerous to oneself and one's social group. Just the recognition of otherness does not imply negative judgment. But, unfortunately, the discomfort we experience when dealing with the stranger often translates into the judgment of the stranger as bad or even evil.

The ambiguity of dealing with the other is inherent in our nature. On the one hand, our primate natures support xenophobia. Primates in the wild do not cooperate with animals from another tribe. Rather, when encountering another tribe the tribe with more strength will kill all males of the weaker tribe. They then will kill all babies so that the females will ovulate soon to be impregnated with the genes of the winning males. No romance here...

At the same time, though, the very fact that our ancestors were able to invite strangers into their midst enabled cultural progress. The strangers, often females seeking impregnation from non-related males, brought with them the knowledge of new technologies and new insights about the world. The tribe who invited them in had the advantage of increasing their knowledge and the efficiency of their tools. Also, when a tribe was known to be welcoming to strangers, many people who did not fit with their tribes would join the welcoming tribe. This meant that exactly the people who did not quite fit the norms, who were thinking and acting "outside of the box" would influence the welcoming tribe whose cultural and technological progress would make them strong and give them the advantage over other tribes.

But what makes a tribe welcoming? What enables their members to overcome the xenophobia of their very primate nature to welcome the stranger in? According to Robert Bellah[10], it was the development of religion that caused the shift in hominid behavior. Anthropologists understand religion as "a system of symbols that, when enacted by human beings, establishes powerful, pervasive, and long-lasting moods and motivations that make sense in terms of an idea of a general order of existence."[11] The symbols are enacted in rituals and meaning-giving narratives.

For Bellah, the pervasiveness of symbols makes pre-lingual religion most unlikely as symbols depend on the development of language. This, in turn, means that religion evolves in hominids at a fairly late stage. And one element of early religions was the embracing of the other, the stranger, a guest. Even most religions today have embedded in them the love for the other in their otherness. In the sermon of the Mount, Jesus calls us to love our enemies. As we will see in Manfred Oeming's paper

*"As Clear as God's Words"?—Dealing with Ambiguities in the Bible*, for the Hebrew Scriptures the openness to the stranger is crucial. The stranger is a mirror in which we recognize ourselves. But even in the Hebrew Scriptures where many parts are written or redacted in light of the experience of the diaspora, do we find the opposite point of view as well where the stranger is rejected and relegated to an outsider status.

Religions also tend to embrace the reality of ambiguity. Even beyond the myth of "the Fall," ambiguous structures are inherent in most religions. Peter Heinegg in his book review *Do They Contradict Themselves? Very Well Then They Contradict Themselves. Adam Kirsch. The People and the Books: 18 Classics of Jewish Literature* points out the many contradictions within Jewish teachings. The very fact that the Rabbis set before the creation story in Genesis 2 another creation story influenced by their Babylonian surroundings (Gen 1) demonstrates how much they embraced ambiguity.

The understanding of the Bible as God's word and, yet, a collection of historical documents is ambiguous. And Christianity embraces as the founder of their religion a man, Jesus of Nazareth, who was never part of their religion but, rather, lived and died as Jew. Dogmatic constructs like the Trinity and the dual nature of Jesus as the Christ (true human and true God) add additional ambiguity to the very tenets of Christianity. Such ambiguity reinforces the feeling of estrangement when practicing religion and invites the practitioner to embrace the certainty of faith—in the Abrahamic religion the faith in a creator God in whom ambiguity and estrangement is overcome.

This means, religions can offer a life without ambiguity; through faith and commitment, ambiguity and estrangement is overcome. However, human nature still remains. And even if religious eschatology might offer us future or momentary relief from all-present ambiguity, religious dogma can also be used and has often been used to create a false sense of certainty over ambiguity. Phil Corlett in his paper *Belief and Delusion as Palliative Responses to Uncertainty* analyzes some of the underlying brain structures that cause such behavior.

He at first introduces the well-known concept of *cognitive dissonance* as "the internal discord felt from holding conflicting beliefs simultaneously." One would assume that most people, when experiencing cognitive dissonance, will give up beliefs and assumptions in order to make their perceived reality more cohesive. However, in a majority of cases this doesn't happen. Rather, humans tend to display confirmation bias "in which prior beliefs bias current decision making, specifically, contradictory data are ignored if they violate a cherished hypothesis." At first, this seems counterintuitive. Why would our brains have evolved to believe even in face of obvious contradictions? What could be the adaptive advantage? Corlett cites as one example New England Puritans. By not allowing any doubt and any dissent, they could focus all their strength on survival and building a sustainable colony.

Certainty as advantage of survival can have unintended consequences that go far beyond religious fanaticism and intolerance. Political partisanship is another prime example. Such partisanship and the rejection of members of the other party and their points of view is nothing new. However, as Ben Gross in his paper *More Choice, Less Uncertainty: The Paradoxical Relationship of Political Identity and News Exposure in the American Public Sphere* points out, the Internet has increased the possibility to find likeminded people and avoid people with different opinions altogether. Selective exposure to news creates different and incompatible realities that are nonetheless attractive because of their non-ambiguity. As he writes, "social attitudes of political partisans seem very strong, stable, and virtually impervious to change. These traits reduce the ability to appreciate the presence of ambiguity in the political beliefs held by others. While differing political viewpoints and theoretical assumptions are central to a healthy Democracy, an inability to recognize and validate the varying worldviews held by others is problematic."

Different groups adhere to different truths and live in different realities. Dialogue seems impossible as there is no common language. Even if all groups formally speak American English, they use words with a wide array of connotations and can therefore not exchange ideas, and no group seems to actually understand what the other group attempts to convey.

Ambiguity avoidance is made possible and then reinforced by the select exposure of the Internet which enables us to live in a world of clarity and without ambivalence and uncertainty because it enables us to be selectively exposed only to those viewpoints that mirror our own. And since our desire for clarity seems to have had an adaptive advantage, it is very hard to overcome.

And, yet, there are many people who actively seek out ambiguity. If we go back to the Biblical origin of estrangement, we will see that judgment and categorization are functions for overcoming ambiguity and randomness. Without categorization, there would be no science, no understanding of our world. But without judgment, there also wouldn't be any art. Senses help us to survive in dangerous and unpredictable environments. But we humans also judge our sensual impressions and go out of our way to create positive sensual input. Other animals also seek out pleasurable experience but humans seem to be the only species using creativity to create experiences that are sensually pleasurable. We create rhythms for the pleasure of dancing, music for the pleasure of our ears, soft materials for pleasing our skin. Perfumes please our noses and cooking both our sense of taste and smell. And so is art the final example for ambiguity. Tobi Kahn's cover art resembles a gestalt image such as the face–vase picture. Do we actually see two islands? And are these islands connected by the river or does the river separate them?

As he writes in his accompanying paper: "My work is abstract, and yet always relates to the physical world, its grandeur and simplicity. I have tried to create work that seems unaffected by time, but at the same time, I am aware of time's passage, the possibility of loss, an abrupt reversal of safety. In the face of the world's instability, I want to reveal the elemental." And, yet, as he also points out, his creativity can best be understood in light of the Holocaust in which numerous of his family members were murdered. And the Holocaust is yet another, unfortunate, result of the desire for ambiguity avoidance, where a culture judges other cultures, other rituals, other religions as bad, refutes the reality in which these people live, and strives for a unified culture. Nazi-Germany resembled the New England Puritans on a giant scale.

Another example of cultural oppression and the rejection of otherness also forms the background for Brett Esaki's paper *Japanese American Spiritual Ambiguity and Arts of Silence*. He describes the emergence of the Japanese free jazz movement. "Free jazz does not have rigid musical structures and has a sharp edge that directly expresses the emotions and contradictions of life under marginalization and oppression" and often reflects "on the injustices of the internment camps and anti-Asian racism, while embodying a freedom to protest, to enact cultural forms, and to express a variety of ambiguous experiences." Exposed to this music in a classroom, Asian-American students tended to find the lack of form and direct emotion true to their experience while most other students were confused and didn't like this confusion. Art as a way to express ambiguity and, indeed, revel in it as it reflects one's own feelings of alienation back and gives it validity.

And Esaki finishes his piece with a strong statement that might as well serve as the conclusion of this introduction. "Ambiguity can cultivate empathy, irresolution can breed courage, and silence can embody security."

As Oeming points in his conclusion, not every person is capable or willing to accept ambiguity. But when we are encouraged to accept ambiguity into our lives, we will be able to celebrate it. In this sense, this volume might serve to celebrate all ambiguities expressing and representing the manifoldness of creation.

**Notes**

1. "Ambiguity." Richard Robinson. *Mind*, Vol. 50, No. 198 (April 1941), 140–155, p. 140.
2. Ibid., p. 143.
3. See "Ambiguity Aversion and the Preference for Established Brands." A. V. Muthukrishnan, Luc Wathieu, Alison Jing Xu. *Management Science*, Vol. 55, No. 12 (December, 2009), 1933–1941.
4. See "Ambiguity in Asset Markets: Theory and Experiment." Peter Bossaerts, Paolo Ghirardato, Serena Guarnaschelli and William R. Zame. *The Review of Financial Studies*, Vol. 23, No. 4 (April 2010), 1325–1359.
5. "Do ambiguity avoidance and the comparative ignorance hypothesis depend on people's affective reactions?" Enrico Rubaltelli & Rino Rumiati & Paul Slovic. *J Risk Uncertain*, Vol 40 (2010), 243–254; p. 244.
6. "Systematic Theology, Vol. 1." Paul Tillich. (Chicago: University of Chicago Press, 1951).
7. "Interacting Minds – A Biological Basis." Chris D. Frith, Uta Frith. *Science*, Vol. 286 (Nov 26, 1999), 1692–1695.
8. "Is Face Processing Species-Specific During the First Year of Life?" Olivier Pascalis, Michelle de Haan, Charles A. Nelson. *Science*, Vol. 296 (May 2002), 1321–1323.
9. "Grooming, Gossip, and the Evolution of Language." Robin Dunbar. (Cambridge: Harvard University Press, 1996).
10. "Religion in Human Evolution." Robert Bellah. (Cambridge: Harvard University Press, 2011).
11. Ibid., Introduction (E-book edition).

## ABOUT THE COVER ART

Tobi Kahn

The art for the cover of Cross Currents on ambiguity reflects my understanding of what it means to be an artist. Since the age of six, I knew I wanted to be an artist. Born into a German Jewish family with a rich cultural and religious history of many generations that were abruptly ended by the Holocaust, I could not distinguish between my vision and my heritage. I stood at my bedroom window for hours in Washington Heights, riveted by the passing world.

My parents and grandparents, all refugees from Germany, honored creativity. We attended museums, concerts, and the theater. Our grandfather took my sister and I for long walks in Fort Tryon Park to explore nature. My sister was named for our murdered aunt and I was named for our uncle, a medical student and artist who, in 1933, was one of the first Jews killed by the Nazis. The knowledge that European Jewry was annihilated continues to shape me.

Other elements contributing to my art have been the birth of my children, the landscapes that I inhabit, cells and biomorphic images: All appear in my work, but are transmuted into archetypes, referring and responding to reality—twenty-first-century experience rendered into a timeless essence.

To create art is an act in the image of the Creator, whose materials are light and darkness, generative and reflecting luminosities, and their attendant color and shadow. Art begins in the capacity to see, a mode of knowing the world and its Maker that is indispensable for religious and cultural expression.

Although Judaism places emphasis on words and interpretation, I find the visual elements of the tradition most illuminating. The name of the Tabernacle's chief artist, Bezalel, means "in the shadow of God," for Bezalel's work is understood to be divinely inspired.

In Judaism, the divine presence is abstract, incorporeal, without beginning or end. The infinite and the finite can meet in spaces designated as liminal, dwelling places that invite our spirit, made in the Image, to encounter the ineffable God in both splendor and intimacy.

My work is abstract, and yet always relates to the physical world, its grandeur and simplicity. I have tried to create work that seems unaffected by time, but at the same time, I am aware of time's passage, the possibility of loss, an abrupt reversal of safety. In the face of the world's instability, I want to reveal the elemental.

The images I create are meant to suggest the paradox of our lives: what we remember is continually being transformed by our imagination, turning the past into dreams that become guides to the way we live.

# CROSSCURRENTS

# JAPANESE AMERICAN SPIRITUAL AMBIGUITY AND ARTS OF SILENCE

Brett J. Esaki

The current political climate is not new. My Japanese American ancestors walked a similar path of uncertainty, and I am listening to them. In my early years, they told me about their experiences and today they continue in spirit, yet their messages have not resonated fully until the last decade or so.

Some of these lessons are straightforward and stated. For example: Imperial powers live in a bath of fear, developing fantasies of hidden pirates and saboteurs and lashing out when the phantoms seem to take form. Imprisoning and banning whole classes of people out of phantom military necessity is not necessary, extremely expensive, and nearly impossible to reverse. Creativity, strength, and endurance are essential for resisting and surviving another's nightmares. The rest of the messages are ambiguous and silent.

My ancestors did not have as many educated and empowered representatives, so they cannot fully guide my path. I count myself among those who have benefitted from my ancestors' perseverance, and I turn to women, African Americans, and Native Americans who can help me to fill in the gap of experience (and listening to others is part of my ancestors' wisdom). In addition to the clear lessons and non-existent ones, my ancestors send silent messages of ambiguity.

Esteemed Japanese American theologian Fumitaka Matsuoka explained that ambiguous messages like these come from Japanese Americans' "holy insecurity," which he later phrased "holy amphiboly." In this article, I will apply Matsuoka's holy amphiboly to the struggle of Japanese

American artists to express messy, contradictory, and ambiguous realities in their art. Artists do so purposefully and sometimes in order to negotiate the political minefield of audiences who do not want to hear direct stories of injustice. By exploring instances of silent ambiguity, I hope to articulate some of the complicated messages of Japanese Americans who have survived times like ours.

**Ambiguity of Japanese American history**

It is accurate to say that the history of Japanese Americans is ambiguous. Our first immigrants were well educated (in respect to the time), hardworking, and with low criminality rates, yet spit on and accused of monopolizing (read "invading") industries and enslaving women. The next generation, born in the United States as American citizens, were categorized as enemy aliens and imprisoned *en masse* (the Internment Camps during WW II). The following generation successfully secured reparations for their parents' losses, yet were depicted as the model minority and symbols of Japan's rise in technology. I am part of the generation after that, and the results are yet to come.

Scholars have commented on the precarious position of Japanese Americans. In the early twentieth century, sociologist Robert E. Park presented Japanese Americans as a prime example of his theory, the Marginal Man, or one who is in transition to assimilation but is held from full assimilation by oppression. Other examples from the 1920s included Jews and mixed-race African Americans.[1] A more recent theory is racial triangulation, where Asian Americans serve as models of economic success through hard work and as rhetorical discipline of stagnant or downwardly mobile African Americans. At the same time, Asian Americans are categorized as foreigners, rendering them incapable of reaching whiteness.[2] Likewise, there has been a common trope among Japanese Americans that we are suspended between white and black. These characterizations of Japanese Americans have utility in some respects and shortcomings in others, yet they all describe the straightforward fact that our lives are ambiguous.

Given this fact, one might ask: Why haven't people just stated that and built from this point? The answer is that there have been countless Japanese Americans who have done this, but it has been difficult for people to understand, especially considering the challenge of understanding ambiguity, as others in this journal attest. In reaction to severe tragedies and minor misfortunes, Japanese Americans used the expression "*shikata ga nai*," which is frequently translated as "it can't be helped." More accurately, it is "what happened is nothing" or "do not dwell on that and move on." More colloquially, it is "sh*t happens" or "shake it off" (in the lyrics of Mariah Carey and Taylor Swift). Presently, I offer that instead of a form of denial or a suggestion to have a short-term memory, "*shikata ga nai*" means "life is ambiguous." Theologically, the phrases "the Lord works in mysterious ways" and "*Namu Amida Butsu*" can work the same way; this life is ambiguous, know this, and move on.

Japanese American artists have also created artistic statements that Japanese American life is ambiguous. Throughout researching my book on silence as a nexus of Japanese American religion, art, and political awareness, I encountered such statements.[3] Avant-garde artists, in particular, illustrated American life with a mixture of joy, tradition, and trauma, and utilized silence because it embodies this multiplicity well. However, the American public largely does not understand this contemporary art. In response, some artists sought to make political statements that others might more easily understand and added didactic descriptions of oppression onto their complex art. However, the American public disapproves, fears, and protests statements that seem to contest American Exceptionalism. In response, to soften the bluntness of political statements, some transformed the messages into hard-to-comprehend modern art, adding an external silence of incomprehensibility that protects the underlying silent messages. The present article explores these related processes of making artistic statements about ambiguity and making political statements seem ambiguous, and illustrates that both match the ambiguous history of Japanese Americans and both utilize silence for their respective purposes. The theological analysis of Fumitaka Matsuoka on ambiguity will be used to articulate the spiritual power of this art, silence, and ambiguity itself. We turn to his theory first.

**Matsuoka's theology of ambiguity: holy amphiboly**
In Matsuoka's well-read *Out of Silence*, he argues that Asian Americans do not find a sense of home in Asia or America and thus find themselves to be sojourners or nomads. As forever wanderers or strangers (to use his

theological terms), Asian Americans develop broad senses of compassion and empathy for others who have undergone similar experiences of oppression, war, and exile. In this way, the love and value of humanity emerges out of the dark depths of experience—a "holy insecurity" as he states in his book and "holy amphiboly" as he more recently writes—or a kind of sacred way of living that comes out of silence.[4]

Before detailing holy amphiboly, it is important to note that this theory of Asian American religion is rooted in Matsuoka's own Japanese American experience. He first immigrated as a college student and quickly learned about American racial marginalization and in turn the experience of other Japanese Americans and other Asian American ethnicities. Based on his background, he truly understands the struggles of the wanderer and stranger. His use of the term "sojourner" was not invented but a common term for early Japanese laborers who originally set off to make money and return home to Japan. However, once arriving and deciding on staying, or not being able to afford return travel, the immigrants found themselves in the ambiguous situation noted earlier. Hence, sojourner still made sense as a description of Japanese American immigrants, continuing through generations of provisional acceptance and rejection. In this way, the concepts of holy insecurity and holy amphiboly are meant to describe the spiritual orientation of perpetual ambiguity.

While living out holy amphiboly, Matsuoka explains that the empathy fosters a rich hybridity with multiple religions. Holy amphiboly is "an experience of a non-singular vision with an unresolved state of non-complimentary cosmologies and faith traditions existing within a person or in a community" and an amphibolous faith is "the simultaneous existence of radically different epistemological and cosmological orientations in a person or in a community."[5] That is to say, holy amphiboly is a state of continually adding new spiritual ideas; this state reflects the perpetual insecurity of Japanese Americans and this cultural hybridity emerges from their social connection to multiple groups through politics, material needs, art, and common experiences. It is the embrace of "irresoluteness, disruption, and even uncertainty" as well as a "respect [for] that which we do not understand."[6] Though painful, perpetual ambiguity has taught Japanese Americans to remain open to others, to discover strength in wells of insecurity, and to develop spirituality and art that directly conveys multiplicity and hybridity. This is a deep, resonant, and productive state of silence. I investigated some of this spirituality and art and discovered that silence has been used to capture the experience of ambiguity.

**Silent art, silent negotiations**

Like Matsuoka articulates a theology of ambiguity, Japanese American artists have been expressing ambiguity in their art, and often use silences to do so. My conception of silence is not restricted to absences, such as the absence of speech or words, but encompasses other cultural conceptions of silence. In my larger study of Japanese American silences, I discovered that Japanese Americans have developed diverse forms of silence based in Japanese conceptions of silence that have hybridized with ideas from other racial, ethnic, and religious groups. Examples of these silences include hiding in plain sight, sensing others' presence, creating a zone of respect, an intense mental focus, recognizing the recurrence of cycles of time, and remembering the lessons of trauma. Thus, silence well embodies the hybridity and internal contradictions of Japanese Americans who are connected to multiple racial, religious, artistic, and political groups. Silence has come to express this manifold multiplicity in part because it has been used to preserve spiritual resources from persecution; by cloaking practices and beliefs under a silent veil of seemingly harmless art and kind culture, these external silences merged with the underlying silences of religion, trauma, and fortitude. Silence has also been a convenient form of artistic expression, because silence matches Orientalist expectations for mysterious Eastern culture. In these ways, silence has become a vehicle for the preservation of religion, culture, and communal history in a society that thrusts ambiguity upon Japanese Americans.

I also discovered that the silences of Japanese American artists have not necessarily been understood by the American public. This was partly on purpose so that those fearful of Japanese people and culture would not notice encoded messages of survival and resistance. Nonetheless, the relative incomprehensibility of ambiguity and silence has led to social and economic issues for Japanese American artists. The examples of jazz artists and sculptors discussed below negotiate this political landscape with varying results, some leading to a decrease in silence and ambiguity and others shifting ambiguous silences.

The difficulty with ambiguity in music is well noted in an anecdote of music scholar Deborah Wong.[7] Wong hosted an avant-garde, free jazz performance in her classroom by Francis Wong and Glenn Horiuchi, two foundational figures in the Asian American jazz movement. They performed several free jazz improvisations, including a particularly dramatic piece on "anthems" including "The Star Spangled Banner." Free jazz does not have rigid musical structures and has a sharp edge that directly expresses the emotions and contradictions of life under marginalization and oppression. The political goal of Wong's and Horiuchi's music was to reflect on the injustices of the internment camps and anti-Asian racism, while embodying a freedom to protest, to enact multiple cultural forms, and to express a variety of ambiguous experiences. Political goals of empowerment and revealing subjugated knowledge have long been part of the Asian American free jazz tradition, which can be traced to 1960s cultural nationalism when jazz musicians represented a fusion of the Asian American Movement with Black Nationalism. Japanese American jazz musicians like Russel Baba, Anthony Brown, Glenn Horiuchi, Mark Izu, Gerald Oshita, and Paul Yamazaki embraced this political edge of their music and many added Japanese instruments and aesthetics for a unique blend of Japanese American music. In addition to the preservation and mixing of cultures and the advancement of political goals, the experience of World War II internment has been a frequent theme of Japanese American musicians, and these layers combine for powerful ambiguity.

Returning to Deborah Wong's anecdote, after the performance she had students describe their reactions. Some Asian American students responded that the lack of form and direct emotion was true to their experience; this is the main goal of the performance of ambiguity and the silences of injustice and of Asian and African American music. Asian Americans and non-Asian Americans alike described their reactions as confused, though some non-Asian Americans interpreted their confusion as "irritating."[8] To use Matsuoka's terminology, the musicians conveyed the state of irresolution, disruption, and uncertainty—the complicated emotions of sojourner existence—yet with energy to express how this state empowers radical openness and courage. The music mixed pain with joy (a blues emotion) drew upon spiritual resources of Asian American and African American religions and political movements, and Matsuoka explains that this active incorporation is part of holy amphiboly and is meant to inspire empathy and an embrace of what is not understood. Asian Americans in the audience seemed to understand these multilayered silences of trauma, hiding, strength, and love, and thus these students engaged holy amphiboly. However, those complex messages were often lost, and a significant number of the audience left annoyed and did not feel inspired toward empathy.

In light of these reactions by many without a similar Asian American experience, it should be no surprise that many Japanese American jazz artists choose to make more direct, less ambiguous political statements that others can understand. Through introductory speeches or poetry read over the track, Japanese Americans have made the history and reasons for the emotions clear, instead of the amorphous sounds of free jazz. For example, fusion jazz group Hiroshima wrote "Living in America" that describes the struggles of Japanese Americans and internment and their album *Third Generation* contains songs of encouragement for Japanese Americans, such as "Do What You Can."[9] Another example is Anthony Brown's collaboration with San Jose Taiko (a Japanese American drumming group from San Jose, California) in the album *Big Bands behind Barbed Wire*, which describes jazz bands during the internment camps.[10] In these examples by Hiroshima and Brown, the lessons about Japanese American history are didactic and hold little ambiguity, but the music itself is multilayered with both jazz and *taiko*. The layering is especially empowered by *ma*, which is a Japanese musical aesthetic of silence. *Ma* is prevalent because *taiko* focuses on *ma* and Brown even wrote a master's thesis on it. In these ways, the complex emotions are there but more as a foundation to the experience of the music. On the other hand, the words tend to direct the listener to locate the emotions in a specific political framework, effectively rendering the emotions less irresolute and uncertain.

One might argue that the clarity of the political message and origins of the emotions increases the reach of holy amphiboly, given that potentially confused audiences would at least be provided with a means of interpretation. Instead of leaving with annoyance like much of the audience in Wong's class, listeners might find a way to connect to the emotions and become empathetic. On the other hand, audiences that are less irresolute, disrupted, and uncertain are not truly placed in the precariousness of the Japanese American experience. Instead of the radical openness of holy amphiboly, they are likely open to the degree that they agree with the political message as framed by the lyrics. That is to say, the reduction of ambiguity comes at a cost of a reduced holy amphiboly, or the deep silence has been silenced. What is gained is a number of people who are introduced to the fact that the historical events happened. With basic recognition, they take a first step toward empathy, and this basic empathy can be an opportunity to engage the silences and the "non-singular vision" that is communicated in the deeper layer of multicultural and multiracial music.

Reducing ambiguity through clear political messages can be an effective way to reach a broader audience, yet Japanese American artists who use didactic statements often encounter audiences who object to the political messages. Sculptor George Tsutakawa encountered this when he was creating a monument to the Japanese American experience. Tsutakawa was interned in his thirties and he volunteered to serve in the Army. Like other *kibei* (those born in the United States and educated in Japan), he fought at the Pacific Front. He even became a Japanese language teacher to officers. After the War, he continued as an artist, and later in his career in 1983 he created a large sculpture to be placed at the former location of the Puyallup Assembly Center in Portland, Oregon. During the internment events, assembly centers temporarily imprisoned Japanese Americans while the larger internment camps were constructed. The Puyallup Assembly Center held many Japanese Americans in the Pacific Northwest, and Tsutakawa was born in that region. Tsutakawa's original design of the sculpture illustrated adults and children carrying their possessions in luggage, and this was a direct reference to the maximum of two bags permitted to internees for all the possessions they could bring. For those passing by the sculpture, one would be able to see in the demeanor of the people that this was an injustice and furthermore the audience could contemplate what it would be like to choose which possessions were most vital to save in their two bags. This is a fairly direct message about the era and also manages to include the silences of great uncertainty, turmoil, and worry.

However, as art historian Martha Kingsbury described, the owners of the land of the former assembly center, though commissioning the sculpture, were worried that this direct message would be placing blame for internment on themselves or other non-Japanese Americans.[11] The owners declared that the sculpture would have to be moved outside of the former assembly center or they would cancel the project. Tsutakawa creatively chose a third option, and that was to design a sculpture that was more abstract. The owners approved of this new design and compromise. The new design still had symbols of Japanese Americans and the bags, but it became sufficiently apolitical with a new layer of silent indecipherability.

In this way, when the political message is too well understood, a general American audience may reject the entirety of the art; thus, they would not even get to the point of recognizing the underlying silences. Whereas jazz artists included didactic lyrics and poetry to convey a clear political message and to inspire empathy from those outside of the Japanese American community, this sculpture could not inspire empathy precisely because those outside of the community understood and objected to the political message. Tsutakawa's tactic of making the piece abstract, effectively adding a layer of silent indecipherability, avoided the political conflict. Now in public, an observer—not rejecting it offhand—may spend an additional amount of time to contemplate the piece, then may feel the silences of turmoil, and then may be inspired to empathize. On the other hand, it may end up in the former problem that a casual observer may be confused and annoyed at the modern art piece, and then not experience the messages of holy amphiboly.

Both of these possibilities came to fruition for a public monument to Japanese Americans created by Robert Murase, *The Japanese American Historical Plaza* of Portland, Oregon. Murase was trained in Japanese landscape design of Zen meditation gardens, and he applied this to the monument to create a fusion of Japanese and Native American religion. Great stones were meant to convey a Native American connection to land and ancient spiritual power, as he has demonstrated in other sculptures. In this vein, the Plaza includes a stone path that is meant to appear like a river, and it is lined with plaques with moments in Japanese American history and poems about those eras. In the center of the Plaza and the stone path/river, there are several large boulders with the names of internment camps written on them. Around these boulders, the river eddies and transitions from flowing, smooth-cut walking stones to jagged, shard shapes. In my reading, the shards indicate the silences of turmoil of the internment years. Additionally, in Zen rock gardens, small stones radiate in smooth concentric circles around boulders; the contrast of jagged and irregular stones with the expectation for even, serene circles further indicates the turbulent power of the internment years, literally disrupting the river's flow of Japanese American history. Another similarity is that the boulders in Zen rock gardens often symbolize holy mountains and their *kami* (spirit), and in this way the internment boulders indicate the spiritual power of that moment in history, which is intensely disruptive. In sum, the silence of this central section of the Plaza is one of turmoil and awe. In respect to holy amphiboly, as one silently walks and reflects on the path, one experiences the state of irresolution, disruption, and uncertainty, and one develops empathy. Moreover, the path of history does not stop at internment, but continues further toward reparations and ends in an opening to the future. This continuation and open future demonstrates fortitude, a sense of unresolved possibility, and a respect for what is not understood. By walking the stone path of Japanese American history, one is supposed to enter these silences of Japanese American past, present, and future, to feel complex emotions, and to emerge with empathy.

These experiences are ideal for the visitor, but on occasion the silences have not been understood and reinforced. For example, during the opening dedication ceremony patriotic messages for the United States and Japan were central. The area behind the internment boulders is raised, and dignitaries from the United States and Japan were seated there. In addition to speeches by political figures, local jazz musicians performed "America the Beautiful" and on the river behind the Plaza a fireboat sprayed plumes of water that were red, white, and blue. Note that there are plenty of examples of jazz musicians performing sacred patriotic American songs with irony and the blues, like Francis Wong and Glenn Horiuchi did with one of their pieces mentioned above. I know the vocalist for the dedication ceremony and she embodies much of this irony, being a former internee herself. She also embodies the multiplicity of holy amphiboly, given that she is multiethnic (Japanese and Chinese American) and is a jazz performer. However, even if she performed full of contradiction and empathy, it would probably literally be drowned out by the patriotic fireboat and praise of political figures. Consequently, the mainstream political message may have dominated the silent narrative of the Plaza, rendering it less ambiguous and less silent.

By contrast, a more recent twenty-fifth anniversary performance was, like some of the jazz with didactic political messages, direct about the pain that undergirds the Plaza's design. For example, actor and political activist George Takei gave a speech about his experiences as a child in internment—a mixture of childhood joy among friends and family while under adult intimidation of armed guard towers. Additionally, a local community swing band forged in honor of the band at the Minidoka Internment Camp performed at this ceremony. Essentially, this performance matches the power and problems of jazz music with lyrics of didactic political statements.

To recap, a clear political statement by Tsutakawa was made ambiguous, and Murase's ambiguous art was transformed into a patriotic political statement without ambiguity and later into a political statement of ambiguity. Likewise, the jazz music has oscillated from incomprehensibility and direct emotion to clarity and background emotion. With all of these degrees and permutations of ambiguity, it is clear that Japanese American artists remain dedicated to expressing Japanese American struggle with silences, and in the above examples we focused on the silences and turbulence of the internment years. Artists also remain dedicated to ambiguity, whether it be the mixed cultures and emotions of a permanent sojourner state or it be the uncomfortable underlying experience in music and sculpture that can be accessed after the external political message hooks one in.

### Holy amphiboly in a time of ambiguity

We are left with a conundrum, or perhaps irresolution. Fumitaka Matsuoka argues that Japanese Americans have experienced this ambiguity for their entire American experience, yet it has not destroyed the community but undergirded it with radical openness and a broad sense of empathy. It is perhaps this desire to deepen their connection to a broad audience (to which they already feel connected) that they choose to include didactic political messages. Further, lyrics, poetry, historical documents, and historical facts add another layer of art and culture to the underlying art form, such as music and sculpture. In this light, it may be more authentically ambiguous to include a somewhat contradictory message on top of the irresolute art—a kind of external disruption to match the internal disruption of Japanese American life. Silences then increase exponentially with: political silences mentioned in the words that layer on top of the artistic silences; religious silences of meditation and disruptive *kami*; and, historical silences of trauma and irony that cannot be explained. This is a sacred "non-singular vision" or holy amphiboly.

On the other hand, the didactic statements in some ways mute the underlying silences; listeners are directed to categorize the cultural mixtures and complex experiences in specific political frameworks. Thus, the words authorize a listener to ignore or to reject the silences if the listener objects to the politics. This is social silencing of a message about social silencing as well as the other underlying silences of art, religion, and communal history. For many who dedicate themselves to the modern, abstract, and directly emotional art, this potential problem is not really a issue because they are not concerned about communicating to a wide audience, so they will not include simple-to-understand words. Instead, they are dedicated to pulling out a listener's empathy, because how can one come to respect the complexity of experience without complexity. They sit in their state of irresolution, disruption, and uncertainty in order to inspire *radical* openness and empathy, not a *little bit* of openness and empathy. They want their spirit to talk on a spiritual level. Yet, it is ironic that radical openness might not be open to straightforward words.

Essentially, it seems that these choices of artists—this back and forth, ebb and flow, or dance within ambiguity—are part of what it is to be Japanese American. The permanent sojourner state means that we live in contradiction, but as Matsuoka and I have argued Japanese Americans have direct means of communicating this, like silence. To an ambiguous life, Japanese Americans add ambiguity, whether that is to survive by hiding in plain sight, to connect by hybridizing with many others, to hide a political statement in abstract symbols, or to create irony with clear words on top of silence. To lifetimes full of denials of clarity, we have responded with the courage to remain uncertain, to adopt new spiritual resources, and to love.

I hope this ambiguous message is one that the American public is ready to hear. We live in a time that demands singular purpose, that forgets straightforward lessons about fear, power, and mass incarceration. The fight to have basic lessons of history and primary respect for others is not over and needs to continue to be fought. But, maturity demands engaging with more difficult, nuanced, and complex phenomena; these are also important lessons of Japanese American history, lessons that I am comprehending more each day. Ambiguity can cultivate empathy, irresolution can breed courage, and silence can embody security.

**Notes**

1. Park, Robert E, 1928, "Human Migration and the Marginal Man," *The American Journal of Sociology* 33(6), May, pp. 881-93.
2. Kim, Claire Jean, 1999, "The Racial Triangulation of Asian Americans," *Politics and Society* 27(1), March, pp. 105-38.
3. Esaki, Brett J, *Enfolding Silence: The Transformation of Japanese American Religion and Art under Oppression* (New York: Oxford, 2016).
4. Matsuoka, Fumitaka, *Out of Silence: Emerging Themes in Asian American Churches* (Cleveland, OH: United Church Press, 1995); "Learning to Speak a New Tongue: Imagining a Way That Holds People Together," in *Asian and Oceanic Christianities in Conversation: Exploring Theological Identities at Home and in Diaspora*, ed. Heup Young Kim, Fumitaka Matsuoka, and Anri Morimoto (Amsterdam, Netherlands: Rodopi, 2011), pp. 217-30.
5. Matsuoka, Fumitaka, "Learning to Speak a New Tongue," 227, 226.
6. Ibid, 228.
7. Wong, Deborah, *Speak It Louder: Asian Americans Making Music* (New York: Routledge, 2004), pp. 288-93.
8. Ibid., 294-95.
9. Hiroshima, "Living in America," *East*, CD, 1989, Sony EK45022; "Do What You Can," *Third Generation*, CD, 1983, Epic E25562.
10. Asian American Jazz Orchestra, *Big Bands Behind Barbed Wire*, CD, 1998, Asian Improv 0045.
11. Kingsbury, Martha, *George Tsutakawa* (Seattle: University of Washington Press, 1990), pp. 19-23.

# CROSSCURRENTS

# BELIEF AND DELUSION AS PALLIATIVE RESPONSES TO UNCERTAINTY

Philip R. Corlett

I n December 1954, the Chicago Tribune reported that Dr. Charles Laughead of Michigan foresaw the end of the world via tidal wave and volcano. He was speaking on behalf of Dorothy Martin, who was supposedly relaying a prophecy from extraterrestrials. The prophecy did not manifest. Martin was placed in psychiatric care to avoid legal charges for creating disturbances and scaring children with her prophecies. However, on leaving that care, she traveled to the Peruvian Andes, Mount Shasta, in California and ultimately settled in Sedona, Arizona, where she lived until she was 92, continuing to proselytize about aliens and their ministrations on earth, but essentially evading interaction with psychiatric services. Did Laughead, Martin, and their followers have delusions? Their beliefs were certainly bizarre and firm. At times, being a follower, sharing those beliefs, was distressing (although that distress usually arose when the beliefs were challenged, rather than when adherents considered the consequences of the beliefs—that the world would end). The beliefs were definitely outside of the doxastic norms of the culture. However, something seems different about these followers compared to the clinical cases with which we are more familiar. One way to explore the overlap and distinctions between belief and delusions is to consider their function. I believe that healthy and unhealthy beliefs are responses to uncertainty or ambiguity. By explaining away the inexplicable, they permit continued engagement with the world.

I define uncertainty and ambiguity in terms of decision-making and probability distributions. We can have uncertainty with regard to a particular event, we can assign it some subjective probability based on what we know and believe. That probability (based on knowledge and beliefs) may be very different between individuals. Ambiguous situations are so uncertain that we do not have enough information to be sure that our particular belief—our specific prediction—is the correct one. In perception, an uncertain situation would involve listening to a friend speak at a noisy party (you can resolve the uncertainty by making predictions based on what you know about your friend). Listening to someone you have just met, at the same noisy party, someone about whom you have no prior beliefs would engender ambiguity. Both are at best frustrating and at worst distressing. We respond to both uncertainty and ambiguity by relying on prior beliefs. And we can respond strongly and sometimes counter-intuitively when those priors themselves are challenged.

Unbeknownst to Martin, some of her followers were imposters: social psychologists, led by Leon Festinger. The academics infiltrated the group as the end-times loomed. The result was a book; *"When Prophecy Fails: A social psychological study of a modern group that predicted the destruction of the world"* (Festinger *et al.* 1956). They developed the theory of cognitive dissonance, the internal discord felt from holding conflicting beliefs simultaneously (Festinger 1962)—in this case, between the prophecy and real world events. People in the cult responded in a variety of ways to reduce their dissonance. Many relinquished their beliefs. In some cases, however, a dissonant experience actually **increased** conviction. For example, failed predictions were recontextualized as actually having come to fruition ("the aliens did come for us, but they were scared off by the crowds of press"). These deft sleights of mind (McKay *et al.* 2005) will be familiar to those who have spoken to patients with delusions (Garety 1991, 1992).

One major challenge for humans is to form and maintain a set of beliefs about the world that are sufficiently accurate and strong to guide decision-making, but flexible enough to withstand changes in the underlying contingencies. One way this might be achieved involves Bayesian learning; we sustain a set of prior beliefs based on past experience, and we combined them with new data. If those new data are highly precise and compelling, they garner updating of the prior. If they are not, those data can be discarded. However, sometimes people do not update their beliefs in this manner. For example, when confronted with evidence that challenges a deeply cherished belief, such evidence may backfire and strengthen people's belief. Is such behavior contrary to the Bayesian model? Furthermore, in the face of uncertainty and ambiguity, people seem to adopt unrelated, sometimes contradictory, and extreme beliefs. This likewise seems to depart from Bayesian rationality. Here, I will describe some of the work and theorizing on belief ad delusion and the palliative function they may both serve with regard to minimizing uncertainty. I will show that while some beliefs appear irrational, they can nevertheless arise from a system that conforms to Bayesian principles.

## Bayesian brains

Hierarchical Bayesian approaches to belief in the brain are simple and intuitive: What we ultimately learn to believe (posterior belief) depends on the integration of previously held beliefs (prior beliefs, priors) with new information (evidence; Friston 2005a, Lee and Mumford 2003). We generate an internal model of the world (and of ourselves as agents who act in it). We use the model to generate predictions that are compared to incoming data. When predictions are violated, a prediction error (PE) signal can update the model. PE may also be ignored, depending on its variance; highly variable PE's tend to be discounted. PEs thus enable a flexible adaptation to changes in the environment (Corlett et al. 2010). Ultimately, the brain works to minimize uncertainty (or PE). It maintains a set of predictive associations (based on past experience) that is flexible enough to adapt yet robust enough to avoid superstitions and instabilities (Friston 2005a, 2009). PE minimization occurs at all levels from the single neuron (Fiorillo 2008) up through the hierarchical neuroanatomy of the brain (Friston 2005a, 2009).

Prior expectations based on established associations are communicated from areas with more abstract representations downwards through the hierarchy (Mesulam 2008). PEs can either be canceled by top-down expectancy (i.e., something unexpected is ignored) or propagated and used to update associations with new learning (Friston 2005a, 2009). Whether PE is ignored or incorporated depends on its precision—consistent errors are precise and drive new learning, imprecise errors are less likely to garner updates. Precision is signaled by specific slower neuromodulators dedicated to the particular inference (e.g., acetylcholine for perceptual inference, dopamine for motor inference). And these slower neuromodulators are implicated in the pathophysiology of psychosis (Adams et al. 2013, Friston 2005b).

I have previously explained delusions, the fixed false beliefs that characterize serious mental illnesses like schizophrenia in terms of these Bayesian mechanisms (Corlett et al. 2007, Hemsley et al. 1994, Miller 1976). Unexplained PE or uncertainty is stress inducing. We do not like being surprised. Explaining surprise so that events can be better predicted in the future drives belief formation. And even if the belief is wrong, or delusional, it still explains away the uncertainty or resolves the ambiguity.

**Bayesian biases?**

This predictive coding model of mind and brain function and dysfunction seems to be committed to veracity; at its heart is an error correcting mechanism that maximizes future rewards and minimizes punishments like the agents of traditional microeconomics—econs (Padoa-Schioppa and Schoenbaum 2015)—theoretical agents whose decisions are only focused on rationally optimizing the expected value. This seems at odds with predictive coding models of psychopathology and in particular psychotic symptoms like hallucinations and delusions (Corlett et al. 2010). Put simply, if delusions result from a noisy maladaptive learning mechanism, why do individuals learn anything at all—let alone the complex and strongly held beliefs that characterize psychotic illness? We know from behavioral economists that humans can depart from econ-like responding (Kahneman et al. 1982). Can predictive coding depart likewise? We think so. Computational modeling of learning and perception allows us to test the consequences of specific changes in a model learner (Stephan and Mathys 2014). For example, some models produce biases— the spreading of erroneous rumors in a social network (Butts 1998), or the tendency to ignore base rates when making probabilistic decisions (Soltani and Wang 2010), even habit formation (FitzGerald et al. 2014).

One particularly interesting example is the confirmation bias (Lord et al. 1979, Nickerson 1998), in which prior beliefs bias current decision-making; specifically, contradictory data are ignored if they violate a cherished hypothesis. At first, it is hard to think that maintaining a belief in the face of contradiction could be adaptive. However, Boorstin (1958) has argued that confirmation bias permitted the seventeenth-century New England Puritans prosper: They had no doubts and allowed no dissent, so were freed from religious argument to focus on practical matters. Their doctrine was so clear and strongly held that they had an all-encompassing explanation (Boorstin 1958). Confirmation bias may save energy and allow work on more pressing tasks. Confirmation bias also protects ones' sense of self as a person with a consistent and coherent web of beliefs living in a predictable world.

The confirmation bias has been tied to striatal PE learning through theoretical and quantitative computational models (Doll *et al.* 2009) as well as genetics (Frank *et al.* 2007, Heyser *et al.* 2000). Confirmation bias is increased in individuals with delusions (Balzan *et al.* 2013). The striatal protein DARPP-32 has been implicated in striatal PE, and risk for schizophrenia (Meyer-Lindenberg *et al.* 2007). On the other hand, Doll *et al.* (2014) found that patients with chronic schizophrenia did not show an enhanced fronto-striatal confirmation bias. The relationship with delusions was not examined. It is possible that confirmation biases are specific to delusion contents (that they are encapsulated) rather than a general deficit. Woodward and colleagues showed delusion-related confirmation biases (Balzan *et al.* 2013).

Examining people's beliefs about themselves and their future reveals other systematic biases. Most people evince superiority illusions, believing they are better and more skilled than most other people, more likely to receive an award, less likely to suffer lung cancer, and less likely to get divorced than their peers (Sharot 2011). It appears that desirable and undesirable information may be used differently to alter self-relevant beliefs (Sharot and Garrett 2016). Again, this seems the antithesis of Bayesian optimality—wherein you updated beliefs in light of new information regardless of how that belief update impacts you, your self-image and well-being.

However, if we allow beliefs to have value in and of themselves, then Bayesian accounts can apply (Sharot and Garrett 2016). Positive beliefs elicit positive feelings, and negative beliefs elicit negative feelings. People thus maintain an optimistic view of themselves and discard negative information. By contrast, when there is no intrinsic or external advantage for holding a belief, asymmetry in updating may be less apparent (Sharot and Garrett 2016). A positivity bias is more likely when information is ambiguous. For instance, when people receive information on how others rated their appearance, the bias is greater than when updating beliefs about self-intelligence after receiving IQ scores (Sharot and Garrett 2016). Attractiveness ratings are more subjective and more open to dispute than relatively objective test scores. There may be more room for personal positivity bias when it comes to attractiveness compared to intelligence.

Overconfidence, ignoring potential negative consequences, in financial traders can lead to market collapses. However, positive overexpectations can reduce stress and improve physical and mental health. In computational simulations overconfident biased agents outperform unbiased, by persevering and claiming resources they could not otherwise attain. Better, but less optimistic, competitors, acquiesce. However, if the costs of errors are raised, overconfidence becomes less adaptive (Sharot and Garrett 2016).

Indeed, not all biases are positive. Personal uncertainty threats (like thinking of a time in one's life when control was lacking) cause compensatory increases in zeal, particularly for self-relevant beliefs (Proulx et al. 2012). Getting spurious feedback about one's academic performance heightens ones' religious conviction (Wichman 2010). Exposure to uncertainty causes participants to increase the extremity and certainty of their convictions about the death penalty and gun control. Furthermore, uncertainty causes people to place a premium on fairness. Participants denied a voice respond most negatively when they first have been made uncertain. Fair process seems to reassure people that the world is an orderly, predicable place when they are feeling uncertain. However, some uncertainty—possibly that which is endogenously generated and experienced with one's own senses, as aberrant prediction errors (PEs), may be reconciled as psychotic symptoms—departures from consensual reality that manifest as hallucinations (percepts without stimulus) and delusions (fixed, false beliefs).

**Delusion formation and maintenance**

In the psychosis prodrome, attention is drawn toward irrelevant stimuli: People report feeling uncomfortable and confused (Kapur 2003, McGhie and Chapman 1961). This may reflect inappropriate PEs. Functional neuroimaging studies of drug-induced and endogenous early psychosis reveal PEs in frontal cortex in response to unsurprising events—PE intensity correlates with delusion severity (Corlett *et al.* 2006, 2007). During prodrome, the stress-mediator cortisol increases by up to 500 percent (Sachar *et al.* 1963). Heightened stress impairs goal-directed learning and promotes inflexible habit formation (Schwabe and Wolf 2009).

In response to this, confusion and stress occur. Delusions appear in an *aha-moment*, and flexible processing is disabled. Habitual responses are preserved and possibly even enhanced (Corlett 2009, Corlett *et al.* 2010). Cortisol falls as delusions crystalize (Sachar *et al.* 1963), forming the delusion is associated with "insight relief" that helps consolidate it in memory. Cortisol rises once more as delusions conflict with reality (Sachar *et al.* 1963). As people recover and relinquish their delusions, cortisol responses normalize (Sachar *et al.* 1963).

While many delusions have upsetting content, they may solve the overwhelming chaos of the prodrome (Kapur 2003), they may be inferences to the best explanation for that chaos (Coltheart *et al.* 2010). Delusions are also remarkably elastic: They expand and morph around contradictory data (Garety *et al.* 1991, Milton *et al.* 1978, Simpson and Done 2002). Of note, patients can learn about other new things (they do not have an all-encompassing learning deficit) and even critically evaluate others' delusions (Rokeach 1964). However, once a delusion is formed, subsequent PEs are explicable in the context of the delusion and serve to reinforce it (Corlett 2009, Corlett *et al.* 2010). Hence, the seemingly paradoxical observation that challenging subjects' delusions can actually strengthen their conviction (Milton *et al.* 1978, Simpson and Done 2002).

**Other theories**

Cognitive 2-factor explanations of delusions try to explain how delusions might arise from brain damage, like a stroke or closed head injury. They posit a perceptual dysfunction (Factor 1), caused by one type of damage, to one region or regions and a belief evaluation deficit (Factor 2), caused by further damage are necessary for delusions. They make this suggestion because some people have Factor 1 damage but they do not have delusions. The logic and evidence here are somewhat questionable. The Factor 1 people may have damage to regions considered Factor 2. However, the theory is influential and simple in its emphasis of the role of perception and belief in delusion formation and maintenance. McKay and colleagues suggested that motivational processes could influence Factor 2 (McKay *et al.* 2007), that wishful thinking could change belief evaluations. On the other hand, people may actually sense things differently as a function of their motivated biases (McKay and Dennett 2009), so motivated beliefs may involve Factor 1 and sampling the data differently depending upon ones' desires.

I believe the two factors, perception and belief, are strongly interrelated (Corlett and Fletcher 2015). Differentiating top-down (belief) and bottom-up (sensation) effects is a challenge, since, in a generative system, top-down and bottom-up effects and processes sculpt one another. Learned biases can alter perception; we see illusory stimuli that conform to our expectations rather than the sensory data incident on the retina (Pearson and Westbrook 2015).

Self-deception is also relevant to delusions. It entails simultaneously believing some proposition (p) and its antithesis (not-p; Sackeim and Gur 1979). Self-deceivers are often unaware of their conflicting beliefs. (Sackeim and Gur 1979). Subjects may be psychologically motivated to state one belief but act according to another (Sackeim and Gur 1979). The relevance to delusions is clear, particularly in regard to the double-bookkeeping in which some delusional patients engage (believing that they are being poisoned but nevertheless consuming food provided to them). Clearly the self-deceptive, double-bookkeeping state is an ambiguous one.

Drazen Prelec and Danica Mijovec-Prelec tested self-deception in the lab (Mijovic-Prelec and Prelec 2010). In their task, subjects first predict an uncertain outcome (the gender of a character from the Korea alphabet), then describe the outcome when they see it. Some subjects (self-deceivers) stick with their initial prediction even when presented a contrary outcome (as if they can't see what's right in front of them). They are more likely to engage in this deception when incentivized for correct prediction. The Prelecs call on an actor-critic model, such as those proposed to explain instrumental learning with PE (Sutton and Barto 1998). For them, the mind is organized into multiple interacting agents, each operating on different information. For the Prelecs, the actor chooses an action and the critic gives that action a score. The critic tries to learn the actors' policy and the actor tries to get the best possible score (perhaps even better than they deserve). This architecture portends self-deception—the actor tries to fool the critic (Mijovic-Prelec and Prelec 2010). In reinforcement learning, the critic learns the environmental states and the actor, an action policy given those states. Prediction errors update the actor and critic—that is, the critic can update the actor's policy in order to maximize future reward. Actor and critic have been localized to different striatal subregions (actor—dorsal striatum, critic—ventral (O'Doherty 2004)).

Gur and Sackeim examined self-deception using galvanic skin response (GSR) (Sackeim and Gur 1979, 1985). GSR is a metric of salience. The skin sweats more in response to or anticipation of salient events. In their examination of self-deception, Gur and Sackeim played individuals recordings of their own voice and others' voices and asked them to decide whether what they were hearing was their voice or another person's. Gur and Sackeim found that when people hear their own voice, they show an increase in GSR response. They found that some subjects made self-deceptive responses, where they misidentified their own voice as another's, despite evincing the GSR familiarity response. They did not recognize having made such errors and were more likely to self-deceive in the laboratory if they also gave self-deceptive responses on a personality scale (endorsing the statements "I have never lied" or "I have never stolen"; which are unlikely to be true).

**What can we do about strong beliefs?**
In the normative approach to delusions that dominates cognitive neuroscience and clinical practice, delusions are conceived of as a symptom to be eradicatedn. However, in describing her own experience of delusions and treatment, Amy Johnson has invoked WB Yeats—suggesting that clinicians and scientists ought to tread lightly in their work, as they tread on patients' delusions (Johnson and Davidson 2013).

The non-clinical situations in which people with radically different belief structures have clashed and come to a resolution may be instructive.

For example, confronting individuals who are against vaccination with reasons that they are wrong can also backfire and strengthen their conviction that vaccines are harmful (Nyhan and Reifler 2015, Nyhan et al. 2013). We, and others, have argued that delusions and other beliefs are often grounded in personal experiences; to the credulous, personal experiences are the most reliable source (Patients often remark "*I know it sounds crazy, but I saw it with my own eyes, Doctor*"). Relinquishing those beliefs on the basis of others' testimony is strongly related to the credibility of the source (Nyhan et al. 2013), for example, do the individuals trying to change one's mind have a vested reason to disagree, like professional status, roles or affiliations? Perhaps large-scale anti-stigma educational activities in mental health have failed because they failed to employ individuals with lived experience to spread the word about mental illness (Corrigan 2012). With regard to the issue at hand, fixed and distressing delusional beliefs, perhaps peer-support might supplement our standard approaches to mollifying delusions. People with lived experience who have recovered from delusions or learned how to manage them might be better at helping their peers with current delusions.

There are other options. Sharot and colleagues used transcranial magnetic stimulation over left inferior frontal gyrus (the prefrontal cortex), to change the activity of the neurons within a few centimeters of the scalp and skull (Sharot *et al.* 2012). This decreased the positivity bias, and people who were stimulated were less overconfident in their own attributes (Sharot *et al.* 2012). This is a proof of principle. We have already discussed how such overconfidence can be adaptive. The importance of the observation is that we may be able to modulate other, less adaptive beliefs. Finally, there are psychological techniques that may help. Following uncertainty induction, people increase their religious zeal (Wichman 2010). However, if subjects engage in a self-affirmation exercise (writing about their positive values and attributes), the impact of uncertainty on religious zeal is mollified (Wichman 2010). This approach has proven useful in depression (Gortner *et al.* 2006). We posit it may have utility for individuals in the prodrome, about to convert to psychosis since it would inoculate against the mounting psychological distress of that state.

With regard to possible drug interventions, antipsychotic drugs tend to block D2 dopamine receptors. While these drugs mollify delusions and hallucinations, they do not do so in all patients, suggesting that other neurochemical mechanisms may be involved. Dopamine neurons do signal prediction errors, However, there is no single prediction or prediction error signal in the brain but rather multiple hierarchies of inference that converge on a coherent multisensory percept {Apps, 2014 #7511}. There are also many ways in which prediction errors may be perturbed—they may be too precise or not be precise enough, the impairment could occur bottom-up (pathologies of the error signal itself) or top-down (problems with priors), and so forth. The effects may not be consistent within a particular hierarchy or across hierarchies. For example, low-level sensory perturbations can have nonlinear effects on belief higher in the hierarchy—that is, weak sensory priors (and increased low-level prediction errors) may render cognitive priors (higher in the hierarchy) more rigid. This seems to be the case in challenging perceptual inference tasks with ambiguous stimuli, but perhaps less so with less demanding inferences [such as the repeated stimulus trains that give rise to the mismatch negativity that is impaired in psychotic states but not in a manner that correlates with symptom severity].

In conclusion then, uncertainty and ambiguity, either internally or externally generated, by the brain and body or the external world can have rather toxic effects on the mind and brain. Beliefs (delusional and no-delusional) form to halt those effects on the individual, resolving the uncertainty and ambiguity. Ultimately though, since the palliative beliefs do not reflect reality, they may but up against it. I the case of overconfidence, this can have some advantages. However, typically aberrant beliefs generate more uncertainty and ambiguity, and thus cause more problems in the long run.

## Works Cited

Adams, RA, KE Stephan, HR Brown, CD Frith, and KJ Friston, 2013, "The Computational Anatomy of Psychosis," Frontiers in Psychiatry **4**, p. 47.

Balzan, R, P Delfabbro, C Galletly, and T Woodward, 2013, "Confirmation Biases Across the Psychosis Continuum. The Contribution of Hypersalient Evidence-Hypothesis Matches," The British Journal of Clinical Psychology **52**(1), pp. 53–69.

Boorstin, DJ, 1958, The Americans: The Colonial Experience, New York: Vintage Books.

Butts, C, 1998, "A Bayesian Model of Panic in Belief," Computational & Mathematical Organization Theory **4**(4), pp. 373–404.

Coltheart, M, P Menzies, J Sutton, 2010, "Abductive Inference and Delusional Belief," Cognitive Neuropsychiatry **15**(1), pp. 261–87.

Corlett, PR, 2009, "Why do Delusions Persist?," Frontiers in Human Neuroscience **3**, p. 12.

Corlett, PR, and PC Fletcher, 2015, "Delusions and Prediction Error: Clarifying the Roles of Behavioural and Brain Responses," Cognitive Neuropsychiatry **20**, pp. 95–105.

Corlett, PR, GD Honey, MRF Aitken, A Dickinson, DR Shanks, AR Absalom, M Lee, E Pomarol-Clotet, GK Murray, PJ McKenna, TW Robbins, ET Bullmore, and PC Fletcher, 2006, "Frontal Responses During Learning Predict Vulnerability to the Psychotogenic Effects of

Ketamine: Linking Cognition, Brain Activity, and Psychosis," Archives of General Psychiatry **63**(6), pp. 611–21.

Corlett, PR, GD Honey, and PC Fletcher, 2007, "From Prediction Error to Psychosis: Ketamine as a Pharmacological Model of Delusions," Journal of Psychopharmacology **21**(3), pp. 238–52.

Corlett, PR, GK Murray, GD Honey, MRF Aitken, DR Shanks, TW Robbins, ET Bullmore, A Dickinson, and PC Fletcher, 2007, "Disrupted Prediction-Error Signal in Psychosis: Evidence for an Associative Account of Delusions," Brain **130**(Pt 9), pp. 2387–400.

Corlett, PR, JR Taylor, X-J Wang, PC Fletcher, and JH Krystal, 2010, "Toward a Neurobiology of Delusions," Progress in Neurobiology **92**(3), pp. 345–69.

Corrigan, PW, 2012, "Research and the Elimination of the Stigma of Mental Illness," British Journal of Psychiatry **201**(1), pp. 7–8.

Doll, BB, WJ Jacobs, AG Sanfey, and MJ Frank, 2009, "Instructional Control of Reinforcement Learning: A Behavioral and Neurocomputational Investigation," Brain Research **1299**, pp. 74–94.

Doll, BB, JA Waltz, J Cockburn, JK Brown, MJ Frank, and JM Gold, 2014, "Reduced Susceptibility to Confirmation Bias in Schizophrenia," Cognitive, Affective & Behavioral Neuroscience **14**(2), pp. 715–28.

Festinger, L, 1962, "Cognitive Dissonance," Scientific American **207**, pp. 93–102.

Festinger, L, HW Riecken, and S Schachter, 1956, When Prophecy Fails, Minneapolis: University of Minnesota.

Fiorillo, CD, 2008, "Towards a General Theory of Neural Computation Based on Prediction by Single Neurons," PLoS ONE **3**(10), p. e3298.

FitzGerald, TH, RJ Dolan, and KJ Friston, 2014, "Model Averaging, Optimal Inference, and Habit Formation," Frontiers in Human Neuroscience **8**, p. 457.

Frank, MJ, AA Moustafa, HM Haughey, T Curran, and KE Hutchison, 2007, "Genetic Triple Dissociation Reveals Multiple Roles for Dopamine in Reinforcement Learning," Proceedings of the National Academy of Sciences of the United States of America **104**(41), pp. 16311–6.

Friston, K, 2005a, "A Theory of Cortical Responses," Philosophical Transactions of the Royal Society of London. Series B, Biological sciences **360**(1456), pp. 815–36.

Friston, K, 2005b, "Hallucinations and Perceptual Inferences," Behavioral and Brain Science **28**(6), pp. 764–6.

Friston, K, 2009, "The Free-Energy Principle: A Rough Guide to the Brain?," Trends in Cognitive Sciences **13**(7), pp. 293–301.

Garety, P, 1991, "Reasoning and Delusions," British Journal of Psychiatry Supplement **14**, pp. 14–8.

Garety, PA, 1992, "Making Sense of Delusions," Psychiatry **55**(3), pp. 282–91; discussion 292-6.

Garety, PA, DR Hemsley, and S Wessely, 1991, "Reasoning in Deluded Schizophrenic and Paranoid Patients - Biases in Performance on a Probabilistic Inference Task," Journal of Nervous and Mental Disease **179**(4), pp. 194–201.

Gortner, EM, SS Rude, and JW Pennebaker, 2006, "Benefits of Expressive Writing in Lowering Rumination and Depressive Symptoms," Behavior Therapy **37**(3), pp. 292–303.

Hemsley, DR, 1994, "Perceptual and Cognitive Abnormalities as the Basis for Schizophrenic Symptoms," in AS David, and JC Cutting, eds, The Neuropsychology of Schizophrenia, Hove, UK: Laurence Erlbaum Associates, pp. 97–118.

Heyser, CJ, AA Fienberg, P Greengard, and LH Gold, 2000, "DARPP-32 Knockout Mice Exhibit Impaired Reversal Learning in a Discriminated Operant Task," Brain Research **867**(1–2), pp. 122–30.

Johnson, A, and L Davidson, 2013, *Recovery to Practice: Dear Amy & Larry*, Available from: http://www.dsgonline.com/rtp/special.feature/2013/2013_05_21/WH_2013_05_21_fullstory.html.

Kahneman, D, P Slovic, and A Tversky, 1982, Judgment Under Uncertainty: Heuristics and Biases, New York: Cambridge University Press.

Kapur, S, 2003, "Psychosis as a State of Aberrant Salience: A Framework Linking Biology, Phenomenology, and Pharmacology in Schizophrenia," American Journal of Psychiatry **160**(1), pp. 13–23.

Lee, TS, D Mumford, 2003, "Hierarchical Bayesian Inference in the Visual Cortex," Journal of the Optical Society of America A **20**(7), pp. 1434–48.

Lord, CG, L Ross, and MR Lepper, 1979, "Biased Assimilation and Attitude Polarization: The Effects of Prior Theories on Subsequently Considered Evidence," Journal of Personality and Social Psychology **37**(11), pp. 2098–109.

McGhie, A, and J Chapman, 1961, "Disorders of Attention and Perception in Early Schizophrenia," British Journal of Medical Psychology **34**, pp. 103–16.

McKay, R, R Langdon, and M Coltheart, 2005, ""Sleights of Mind": Delusions, Defences, and Self-Deception," Cognitive Neuropsychiatry **10**(4), pp. 305–26.

McKay, R, R Langdon, and M Coltheart, 2007, "Models of Misbelief: Integrating Motivational and Deficit Theories of Delusions," Consciousness and Cognition **16**(4), pp. 932–41.

McKay, RT, and DC Dennett, 2009, "The Evolution of Misbelief," The Behavioral and Brain Sciences **32**(6), pp. 493–510; discussion 510-61.

Mesulam, M, 2008, "Representation, Inference, and Transcendent Encoding in Neurocognitive Networks of the Human Brain," Annals of Neurology **64**(4), pp. 367–78.

Meyer-Lindenberg, A, RE Straub, BK Lipska, BA Verchinski, T Goldberg, JH Callicott, MF Egan, SS Huffaker, VS Mattay, B Kolachana, JE Kleinman, and DR Weinberger, 2007, "Genetic

Evidence Implicating DARPP-32 in Human Frontostriatal Structure, Function, and Cognition," Journal of Clinical Investigation **117**(3), pp. 672–82.

Mijovic-Prelec, D, and D Prelec, 2010, "Self-Deception as Self-Signalling: A Model and Experimental Evidence," Philosophical Transactions of the Royal Society of London. Series B, Biological sciences **365**(1538), pp. 227–40.

Miller, R, 1976, "Schizophrenic Psychology, Associative Learning and the Role of Forebrain Dopamine," Medical Hypotheses **2**(5), pp. 203–11.

Milton, F, VK Patwa, and RJ Hafner, 1978, "Confrontation vs. Belief Modification in Persistently Deluded Patients," British Journal of Medical Psychology **51**(2), pp. 127–30.

Nickerson, RS, 1998, "Confirmation Bias: A Ubiquitous Phenomenon in Many Guises," Review of General Psychology **2**(2), pp. 175–220.

Nyhan, B, and J Reifler, 2015, "Does Correcting Myths About the flu Vaccine Work? An Experimental Evaluation of the Effects of Corrective Information," Vaccine **33**(3), pp. 459–64.

Nyhan, B, J Reifler, and PA Ubel, 2013, "The Hazards of Correcting Myths About Health Care Reform," Medical Care **51**(2), pp. 127–32.

O'Doherty, J, 2004, "Dissociable Roles of Ventral and Dorsal Striatum in Instrumental Conditioning," Science **304**(5669), pp. 452–4.

Padoa-Schioppa, C, and G Schoenbaum, 2015, "Dialogue on Economic Choice, Learning Theory, and Neuronal Representations," Current Opinion in Behavioral Sciences **5**, pp. 16–23.

Pearson, J, and F Westbrook, 2015, "Phantom Perception: Voluntary and Involuntary Nonretinal Vision," Trends in Cognitive Sciences **19**(5), pp. 278–84.

Proulx, T, M Inzlicht, and E Harmon-Jones, 2012, "Understanding all Inconsistency Compensation as a Palliative Response to Violated Expectations," Trends in Cognitive Sciences **16**(5), pp. 285–91.

Rokeach, M, 1964, The Three Christs of Ypsilanti, New York: Alfred Knopf.

Sachar, EJ, JW Mason, HS Kolmer, and KL Artiss, 1963, "Psychoendocrine Aspects of Acute Schizophrenic Reactions," Psychosomatic Medicine **25**, pp. 510–37.

Sackeim, HA, and RC Gur, 1979, "Self-Deception, Other-Deception, and Self-Reported Psychopathology," Journal of Consulting and Clinical Psychology **47**(1), p. 213.

Sackeim, HA, and RC Gur, 1985, "Voice Recognition and the Ontological Status of Self-Deception," Journal of Personality and Social Psychology **48**(5), pp. 1365–72.

Schwabe, L, and OT Wolf, 2009, "Stress Prompts Habit Behavior in Humans," The Journal of Neuroscience **29**(22), pp. 7191–8.

Sharot, T, 2011, "The Optimism Bias," Current Biology **21**(23), pp. R941–5.

Sharot, T, and N Garrett, 2016, "Forming Beliefs: Why Valence Matters," Trends in Cognitive Sciences **20**(1), pp. 25–33.

Sharot, T, R Kanai, D Marston, CW Korn, G Rees, and RJ Dolan, 2012, "Selectively Altering Belief Formation in the Human Brain," Proceedings of the National Academy of Sciences of the United States of America **109**(42), pp. 17058–62.

Simpson, J, and DJ Done, 2002, "Elasticity and Confabulation in Schizophrenic Delusions," Psychological Medicine **32**(3), pp. 451–8.

Soltani, A, and XJ Wang, 2010, "Synaptic Computation Underlying Probabilistic Inference," Nature Neuroscience **13**(1), pp. 112–9.

Stephan, KE, and C Mathys, 2014, "Computational Approaches to Psychiatry," Current Opinion in Neurobiology **25**, pp. 85–92.

Sutton, RS, and AG Barto, 1998, Reinforcement Learning: An Introduction, Cambridge, MA: MIT Press.

Wichman, AL, 2010, "Uncertainty and Religious Reactivity: Uncertainty Compensation, Repair, and Inoculation," European Journal of Social Psychology **40**(1), pp. 35–42.

# CROSSCURRENTS

# "CLEAR AS GOD'S WORDS?"—DEALING WITH AMBIGUITIES IN THE BIBLE[1]

Manfred Oeming

### Between guidance and confusion—the discrepancy between expectation and reality

When humans read the Bible, they look for clear guidance. "Teach me your way, O LORD" (Ps 27:11)—the authors of the Psalms consistently pray. In difficult life situations, on the margins, in ambiguity, they expect that God shows them which way to turn. "Make me understand the way of your tenets" (Ps 119:27). In our cultures, influenced by Jewish and Christian traditions, almost everyone might agree that the Bible serves as ethical guideline helping us making hard moral decisions. But how, exactly, does that work?

Human artists create works that are ambiguous and cannot be reduced to one single and unambiguous meaning. We accept this in our daily lives. For instance, when several people look at a painting, they will associate different things—and this is perfectly acceptable. Even more so, art shouldn't be unambiguous but should produce a multitude of different interpretations and reactions. This has been accepted in hermeneutics and aesthetics at least since Umberto Eco's "Postscript to The Name of the Rose" (1984).

But what happens if these multitudes of meaning happen in God's Word? If the Bible is ambiguous? What in secular art is seen as positive and enriching becomes problematic in the realm of the sacred. And even worse: how can we deal with discrepancies and conflicts in the Sacred

Scriptures? What happens when normative texts provide different and even opposing guidelines to important questions?

"The Rabbis say: "What happens when a hammer meets a rock? Sparks fly. Every spark is the result of the hammer hitting the rock but no spark is a singular result." This is similar to the scriptures where one verse can convey many different teachings" (bSanhedrin 24). It seems that they do not have a serious problem with the plurality of interpretations.

But Protestant Theology has continuously taught *claritas scripturae*. According to this dogma, there are four rules: (1) No dogma necessary for salvation can be unclear. (2) The Scriptures explain themselves; if something is unclear, it can be explained by other parts. (3) If the Scriptures seem to be unclear, the reason can be found in human sin and ignorance. (4) The Scriptures are unambiguous because God has authored them and God would never contradict himself. So far the Protestant dogma. However, reality looks very different.

Since the development of the historic-critical method in Biblical interpretation, it has become obvious that the teachings of the Bible are not unified and clear; rather, the Bible contains numerous points of view. Even key themes and key ethical guidelines are ambiguous as can be shown in numerous instances. I will present one example.

### How to deal with strangers within the framework of Old Testament (OT) ethics

A search of all Biblical passages about the ethical approach to strangers will immediately reveal that the New Testament only offers very general advice. "So there is no difference between Jews and Gentiles, between slaves and free people, between men and women; you are all one in union with Christ Jesus" (Gal 3:28). This is a statement about the internationality of the interconnected church without hierarchy. It challenges us to invite all strangers in, which is seen as service to Christ himself (see also Matthew 25:35 "I was a stranger, and you invited me in"). It even becomes a cardinal virtue—"Remember to welcome strangers in your homes. There were some who did that and welcomed angels without knowing it." (Hebrews 13:2)

But our modern discussions about strangers are embedded in the idea of "the nation" and their competing markets. The question "How many foreigners can we accept into our country without endangering out inner peace?" is a complex one. For its answers, we rely on insights from ethics, the law, economics, and psychology. The OT offers some important insights here, since the distinction between oneself and the other, and the difficulty of living as stranger in an often hostile culture are—without exaggeration—the key problems in the history of Israel and the theology and ethics of the OT.

## Three theological arguments for a principal acceptance of the stranger

*The nature of god:* In Deuteronomy, we can find the definitive argumentative structure:

> For the Lord your God is the God above the Gods and Lord of Lords. He is the great God, the Hero and the Frightening one. He shows no partiality and accepts no bribes. He defends the cause of the orphans and the widows. He loves the strangers, giving them food and clothing. And you are to love those who are foreigners, for you yourselves were foreigners in Egypt. (Dt 10: 17–19)

God's nature and being is of utmost importance—also for political and economical ethics. God transcends boundaries; he is the universal God. This highest being is surprisingly embracing of the lowest people. He loves humans in emergency situations: the orphans, women without protection of a husband, and the strangers who don't own land and who don't have securities or rights.

The expression "God loves the strangers" is very strong and memorable. "Love" in Deuteronomy is both a feeling of attachment and commitment that legally binds. This image of God gives orientation as well as the scale of the expected commitment: "You as well should love the strangers." The *Imitatio Dei* is a constitutional law. Israelites know from their own experience what it means to live in an insecure environment; "Egypt" is a code for famine, slavery, and exploitation. Contemporary analyses of Deuteronomy even ask if this part of Deuteronomy 10 does not have a similar function as the *Sch$^e$ma Israel* in Dt 6:4–5—a confession to be repeated daily.[2]

*The nature of humans:* A second ethical argument is rooted in the theology of creation: God has created humans, that is, every human, man and women, in his image (Gen 1:26). All human beings have equal worth.

> Did not he who made me in the womb make them? Did not the same one form us both within our mothers? (Job 31:15)

This and similar passages (see, for instance, Prov 14:31: Whoever oppresses the poor shows contempt for their maker, but whoever is kind to the needy honors God) formulate ethical obligations.

Equally important as the love of God (Dt 6:4) is the love of the neighbor (Lev 19:19). But the logic of the holiness code enhances the scope of the commandment of love by making it transcend religious barriers.

> The foreigner residing among you must be treated as your native-born. Love them as yourself, for you were foreigners in Egypt. I am the Lord your God. (Lev 19:34)

Biblical research assigns the Hebrew commandment *wa'ahabtä lô kämôchä* (Love them as yourself) different meanings. The majority of scholars understand the phrase in the way that the amount of self-love should not be greater than the love for the stranger. Another interpretation reads this phrase as "Love the stranger because he is like you." Even if this meaning is highly unlikely given the grammatical structure here, it still fits the content of this commandment. Those who look at the seemingly other through the eyes of the creator will discover that this other, this stranger with his different skin color, his different customs, and his different religion are ultimately not much different from us. The stranger is the neighbor!

*The nature of humanity and the family ethos:* Even today most of us feel that we need to act toward relatives differently than toward strangers. Every human has a natural, instinctive, and protective attitude toward one's kin. For instance, in one's own family we usually don't charge interest when we lend someone money, and we are more likely to support family members than strangers in emergencies. Many of the Biblical texts now point out that *all* humans are brothers and sisters. This means that the ethos toward one's own kin leads to an impressive dynamic. The creation stories in the Priestly Sources of the Pentateuch in Gen 1 and the Genealogies in Chronicle 1 all attest to the conviction that *all* humans come from Adam and are therefore kin.

In the three great OT law collections—the Covenant Code (Ex 20–22), the Law of Deuteronomy (Dt 13–26), and Holiness Code (Lev 17–26)—we find increasingly strong protections for the strangers. They shouldn't be disadvantaged (Ex 22:20–22). In Deuteronomy, they get the right to keep the Sabbath, and to be paid a 10th of the harvest and the right of gleaning after the harvest (Dt 14:28–29). According to the Holiness Code, the love for the stranger even becomes a theological obligation!

*The historical argument:* In the history of Israel, female strangers are very important for the development of the nation. There is, for instance, Ruth from Moab. Even if according to Dt 2:2–9 and Neh 13:1–3:23–27 no Israelite is permitted to marry a Moab, Ruth marries Boaz in Bethlehem and becomes the grandmother of Kind David.

With these four arguments, the nature of God, the nature of humans, the family ethos, and the historical argument, the way of God seems unambiguous! "In Israel God wanted his people to create such an atmosphere, an atmosphere of loving kindness where strangers could feel at home."[3] The Bible demands an open and tolerant immigration policy, culminating in key prophetic texts such as Isa 19:23–25 ("In that day there will be a highway from Egypt to Assyria. The Assyrians will go to Egypt and the Egyptians to Assyria. The Egyptians and Assyrians will worship together. In that day Israel will be the third, along with Egypt and Assyria, a blessing on the earth. The Lord God will bless them, saying, Blessed be Egypt my people, Assyria my handiwork, and Israel my inheritance") and Isa 56: 6–7 ("And foreigners who bind themselves to God to minister to him, to love God's name and to be his servants, all who keep the Sabbath without desecrating it and who hold fast to my covenant; these I will bring to my holy mountain and give them joy in my house of prayer. Their burnt offerings and sacrifices will be accepted on my altar; for my house will be called a house of prayer for all nations").

*Two theological arguments against a liberal integration of the stranger*

However, despite the positive attitude toward integration of the stranger described above, we can also find in the OT a hard and rigid rejection of the stranger (for instance, in statements made against Amalek, Moab, or Edom). We can also find a fear of losing Israel's identity because of too many foreigners swamping the land,[4] and this attitude is also supported by theological arguments. We find often the argument that strangers will bring a different religion and will challenge the very foundations of Israel; see, for instance, during Solomon's time (1 Kings 11:1–4) or during the Persian phase of Jerusalem (Ezra 9:1–2).

Even if Israel has firsthand experienced the cruel consequences of xenophobia—up to anti-Jewish pogroms—we still find such tendencies in many of the canonical texts. Within the Bible, right in front of the reader's eyes rages a battle, and this battle becomes obvious in two instances.

The term "stranger" seems unambiguous at first, but in Hebrew the terms are ambiguous and contested. The Tora uses at least three terms: *zar* (זר), *nochri* (נכרי), and *ger* (גר).[5] All three have the connotation of distance and threat. A *nochri* is a non-Jewish person who comes into the country for a short period. A *nochri* enjoys absolute hospitality but does not have to follow Jewish law and remains distant from the community. But he is not allowed to worship idols, and this commandment implies three prohibited behaviors: sexual offenses, murder, and the worshiping of other gods. A *ger* is an immigrant who converted to Judaism, a proselyte. However, the term can also connote a person who was always Jewish but isn't home at his current place of living. As day laborer or beggar, he belongs to the lowest class. He is not a foreigner but a fellow Israelite who came from another area.[6] He has to obey norms and laws.

The limits to the welcoming of a stranger are twofold. The own identity cannot be threatened and, more importantly, the own religion cannot be harmed. Especially foreign women are presented as dangerous in the OT not so much because they are foreign but, rather, because they worship idols. For instance, the highly celebrated Solomon still is seduced by his foreign women to worship other gods which is why ultimately his kingdom fails (1 Kings 11:11–16). Ezra and Nehemiah undertake mass divorces (Ezra 9–10, Neh 13:23–27) and insist on the law on endogamy (Tob 4:9) to keep Israel's identity intact.

Increasingly, foreigners are expected to adapt to Israel in some ways (e.g., through circumcision, the observation of the Sabbath, or Kashrut) or need to leave. The commandment "The same laws and regulations will apply both to you and to the foreigner residing among you" (Numbers 15:16) implies both the same rights for the foreigner and pressure to integrate and adapt. They are not supposed to have their own rights and laws but follow the laws of the hosting nation. The more the foreigner is willing to adapt, the more he will participate in the privileges of the

Tora, like debt relief during a Sabbath year or the prohibition of usury (Dt 15:3; 23:20–21).

**How to deal with these ambiguities?**
As demonstrated, the ethics of migration in the Bible is ambivalent. Anyone can focus either on the foreigner-friendly or on the foreigner-unfriendly parts. However, the historic-critical method of interpreting the Bible doesn't allow us to pick and choose to support our own point of view. Rather, every reader is confronted with the spectrum of positions. And this is not just the case for the Biblical attitude toward strangers but also for other moral questions such as economic ethics (there are several interpretations for the usury prohibition), sexual ethics (homosexuality is definitely not seen as only negative), or slavery, and many more.

This leads many of the faithful to reject the historic-critical method; for them, it was more a disaster than gain.

But we cannot retreat anymore to naive positions; rather, we need to read the whole Bible. This is especially true as the historic-critical perspective also clearly shows that all positions have their own historical context. The major differences of the various historical situations prohibit us from applying Biblical ideas and models simply one-on-one to today's political situations.

The antique Israel didn't know about mass migration throughout the globe. They also didn't know about the internet as way to connect with people in faraway home countries. The Bible remains in historical distance and shouldn't be abused this way. We cannot support our own prejudices and opinions with individual Bible passages. Rather, we need to be willing to embrace through exegesis a culture of disagreement which is prevalent in the Bible.

The party behind the foreigner-friendly theological positions behind Ruth, Job, and Jonah stands in fierce contrast to the party of the hardliners, and those theological positions behind the Pentateuch and Ezra. These trends demand strict integration, reject strangers, and by enforcing endogamy allow only marriages within a religion.

No party can simply ignore the position of the other. All arguments need to be heard. *"You should love the foreigner!"* According to the theology of creation, all humans are equally Adam's or Noah's descendants. All parties agree that we cannot step back from the theology of creation—

even the hardliners. Every human being has been created by God, is therefore protected by God, and can claim love. Respect for this dignity, however, does not mean automatically that everyone can live in Israel or can live there and practice his or her own religion.

In the OT collections of law codes, we find several strict laws about how to protect the foreigner. In texts from ancient Egypt, we find passages in which the stranger isn't even accepted as human. Assyrians and Babylonians do not have a lot of consideration for foreigners, and antique Greeks judged every non-Greek as barbarian. This means we have to come to our own conclusions in our own codes of laws.

The Bible challenges us to critically reflect, and such reflection must be done by both the inviting societies and the immigrants themselves. The OT explicitly grants asylum to victims of famine. Today's "Western" nations only grant political asylum. The right to work is a given in the context of the OT which stands in stark contrast to the situation of today's asylum seekers. And such protections do not depend on the stranger's conversion to Judaism.

But to what extent is it allowed to pressure strangers to assimilate? How much do strangers have to adapt to our cultural and societal norms in order to become accepted? The Bible prohibits to have parallel groups to whom different laws apply, and demands a unified code of law for all people. And even if this position stands against our modern tendency to tolerate the convictions and norms of all different people equally, it might still be a worthwhile approach. We have to negotiate how much freedom we grant immigrants to stay true to their own culture and how much we pressure them to assimilate.

In meeting the stranger, we look into a mirror. The face of the stranger who asks for our help allows us to look inside ourselves. Since we can only recognize ourselves through the other in his or her otherness, we depend on strangers for getting to know ourselves. The refugee crisis in Europe and North America has led to self-recognition and the reconsideration of our own values based on our Jewish and Christian inheritance.

The task for the churches is twofold. On the one hand, they have to stand up for the rights of migrants, immigrants, and refugees who are often marginalized and maltreated, and whose rights and dignity are often challenged or even denied. The churches have to stand firm here in support of the foreigners.

At the same time, they shouldn't avoid difficult questions or make a taboo of the questions themselves. They need to openly guide the discussions about the necessity of the extent of assimilation, the cost explosions for our social networks, and the psychological problems for some of the natives that can arise when they don't feel home in their own country anymore. The Bible does not avoid asking these questions and neither should we.

The canon of Biblical texts forces us to continually reflect on difficult questions. Religion becomes a demanding intellectual achievement because of the ambiguity of our core texts. And, unfortunately, not everyone is capable of such an intellectual approach.

**Notes**

1. Translated from German by Anne Foerst.
2. E. Otto: Deuteronomium 1–11. Second Volume: 4,44–11,32, HThKAT, Freiburg i.Br. u. a. 2012, S. 1058–1060.
3. H.-G. Wünch, "The stranger in God's land – Foreigner, stranger, guest: What can we learn from Israel's attitude towards strangers?" Old Testament Essays 27 (2014) 1129–1154, 1150.
4. The German term used here is "Überfremdung."
5. M. Zehnder, Umgang mit Fremden in Israel und Assyrien, BWANT 168, Stuttgart 2005.
6. So Ch. Bultmann, Der Fremde im antiken Juda (FRLANT 153), Göttingen 1993.

# CROSSCURRENTS

# MORE CHOICE, LESS UNCERTAINTY: THE PARADOXICAL RELATIONSHIP OF POLITICAL IDENTITY AND NEWS EXPOSURE IN THE AMERICAN PUBLIC SPHERE

Benjamin Gross

## Introduction

Ambiguity is defined as a situation of inexactness, and is synonymous with the feelings of uncertainty and ambivalence. It is a state of mind that one might generally expect to find when discussing complex social and political issues with others, as the causes of and remedies to societal ills is far from being clear to all citizens. Nevertheless, discourse in the United States has become highly polemic in the early twenty-first century, where the social attitudes of political partisans seem very strong, stable, and virtually impervious to change. These traits reduce the ability to appreciate the presence of ambiguity in the political beliefs held by others. While differing political viewpoints and theoretical assumptions are central to a healthy Democracy, an inability to recognize and validate the varying worldviews held by others is problematic.

How has this occurred in a society where there exists a nearly countless amount of mediums for people to collect and share political information? Is it possible that the ability to share and consume information so readily actually reduces ambiguity rather than increases it? Questions such as these have been addressed by a wide variety of scholars in recent years, cutting across all academic disciplines. This article reviews the literature regarding political news media and its relevance to the rise of attitudinal extremity found among the American public. Additionally, new data will be explored that tests whether media selectivity increases feeling of antipathy and blame that self-identified political partisans hold toward members of the opposing party in the United States.

**Literature review**

In the study of media and politics, a central figure that is widely cited among most scholars is Jürgen Habermas, whose concept of a "public sphere" (1989) is still highly influential. He defines a public sphere as any space where individuals can come together to freely discuss & identify societal problems. Under ideal conditions, according to Habermas, this space is characterized by a wide array of perspectives that are being voiced by citizens coming from all walks of life. While such a situation is not feasible with mass mediums, due to the prohibitively high costs to entry and limited space available (such as the time of television broadcasts and length of newspapers), the Internet would seemingly enhance the public sphere. After all, virtually anyone can access the Internet at a minimal cost, and share his/her opinion as widely as they wish across a wide array of platforms.

Under such conditions, this Habermasian conception of the public sphere should lead people to feel very optimistic about the prospects for Democracy. With such a vast and diverse collective of information readily available to anyone who goes online to learn about and discuss politics, one would expect that American public opinion regarding political issues would generally be defined by complexity and ambiguity today. If Americans were spending considerably large amounts of time each day online, contemplating both conservative and liberal viewpoints and assumptions about societal conditions as they learn, it should be nearly impossible to avoid feelings of ambivalence regarding these problems. However, more often than not, this does not seem to be the end result for most users.

Instead, those who engage in online politics tend to engage in patterns of "selective exposure" (Freedman and Sears 1965), which is defined by a preference of individuals for attending to information that is likely to confirm their pre-existing viewpoints. This concept is highly similar to Leon Festinger's (1957) theory of cognitive dissonance, where people actively avoid disconfirming information due to their dislike of feeling uncertainness or ambiguity. Taken together, these serve as possible explanations for why those who use mass and social mediums for political information develop higher levels of certainty and attitudinal extremity over time.

The research of Joseph Klapper (1960) was the first to relate self-selectivity to media exposure for the purpose of understanding social attitudes. What he found was that media content held only limited effects on public opinion. Klapper's results indicated that people had a strong tendency to engage in selective exposure to information when they already held stable beliefs about a topic. Additionally, it was found that social attitudes tended to become more extreme over time due to the extended repetition of consonant information. In the long-term, when an observable shift of an individual's attitudes occurred, it was more likely in the direction of extremity rather than in the direction of changing his/her opinion to the opposing viewpoint.

While this line of research focused on mass media and user selectivity, a large body of literature has focused on whether these findings are relevant to cyber space. One of the first theories that relate selectivity to Internet activity patterns became known as "Cyber Balkanization" (Van Alstyne and Brynjolfsson 1996). A "Cyber Balkan" Internet user is defined as someone that (1) tends to define their "community" primarily in terms of only those who share their values regardless of physical proximity, (2) prefer to be surrounded by similar others online, and then consequently (3) selectively expose themselves to websites where they expect others to confirm their pre-existing viewpoints. According to this theory, a Cyber Balkan is motivated by a desire to maintain a sense of certainty in their previously held beliefs, tends toward dogmatism, and is likely to express anger toward political opposition.

This early conception of the Internet as a space where personal biases and attitudinal extremity would flourish has found a substantial amount of support from other researchers. Online spaces of political discourse do seem to have a high degree of selective exposure, which was observed clearly in the often cited research of Lala Adamic & Natalie Glance (2005), in their study of the US political blogosphere during the 2004 election. Their research showed that there was a very clear overlap in the exposure patterns of liberal "blue" readers and the more conservative "red" readers, with very little overlap being observed between these two separate constellations of blog networks during the election season.

Similar patterns of partisan selectivity have been found in other research as well (Sunstein 2007, Iyengar and Hahn 2009, Stroud 2011, Gross 2015, Bakshy *et al.* 2015, Keegan 2016). These patterns of selective exposure in political media content are believed to increase the strength of political beliefs and attitudes, increasing polarization among the public (Dahlberg, 2007; Sunstein 2007, Bennett and Iyengar 2008, Iyengar and Hahn 2009, Stroud 2011). Many Internet users seem motivated to construct a "daily me" (Sunstein 2009), hearing primarily only loud echoes of their own voices; which is of questionable value from a democratic standpoint (Sunstein 2007). The Internet, above all, is characterized as a space where personal choice is virtually unlimited, permitting users to easily see exactly what they want to see. Personal volition opens up pathways for individual biases and motivations to achieve attitudinal certainty and reinforcement from like-minded others when people engage in politics online, rather than the pursuits of truth, accuracy, and issue complexity (Stroud 2011; Gross 2015).

Many Internet groups, especially those organized around support for political candidates or policies, are unified by the sense of personal camaraderie or shared values among its members. This drives people to a strong tendency toward group polarization (Myers and Lamm 1976, Sunstein 2009), where being surrounded by like-minded others tends to create attitudinal extremity among the group's members. Politics is becoming increasingly personal and connected to animosity toward communities, friends, families, and neighbors to a higher degree than 20 years ago (Pew Research Center, 2016).

Overall, self-selected communities (both online and offline) intensify fragmentation and breed attitude polarization among members (Hogg 1992, Galston 2004, 2005, Wachbroit 2004, Sunstein 2009, Levendusky 2013). People grow more extreme within homogenous groups as a way to conform, and gain reward and status from the group for being more extreme than the group average, propelling each member to move the whole group further away from neutrality or some centrist point (Bishop 2008, Sunstein 2009, Galston 2005). Recent research shows that a preference to be surrounded by like-mindedness and ideological uniformity has become alarmingly high on both the political left and the right. For example, nearly two-thirds of "consistent conservatives" and half (49 percent) of "consistent liberals" say that most of their close friends share their political views (Pew Research Center, 2014). Specialized communities are constructed to reflect shared interests rather than shared space (Putnam 2000), where any particular philosophy, identity, or ideological perspective reinforces pre-existing worldviews within a narrow range of dialogue and challenge (Vacker 2000, Bishop 2008).

Rather than addressing these dangers to Democracy, online platforms commonly embrace and encourage such user activity. News bias exposure patterns have increasingly become a byproduct of technologies that have conscientiously designed themselves around the principles of selective exposure (Herrmann 2016, Tufecki 2016). These designs are not value free or objective, and are feared to be potentially very dangerous to the public. Increasingly, sites such as Facebook, through the design of their algorithms, purposely show users only information that they are predisposed to "like" in order to give their audience a pleasurable experience. This practice, it should be noted, is not exclusively conducted only by online news sites. Berry and Sobieraj (2014) also identify ways which partisan mass media organizations also select content based on what they believe their audience want to see, which has proven to be a highly profitable business strategy.

Facebook, in particular, has become "centralized online news consumption in an unprecedented way" while hosting an enormous amount of political discourse during the 2016 US Presidential election (Pew Research, June 22, 2016). Due to the combination of personal selectivity and an architecture of reinforcement, partisan news sites have thrived on Facebook. These sites, which often spread party propaganda, as well as varying forms of "fake news," often amass huge audiences on parallel with major television news networks. They typically consist nearly entirely of loyal partisan followers, contributing to a rise of anger and ignorance among the public (Putnam 2000, Galston 2005, Manjoo 2008, Pew Research, June 22, 2016). These findings are supportive of the more "dystopian" viewpoint of online politics and selection-based communities (Putnam 2000, Vacker 2000, Katz and Rice 2002, Galston 2005, Nie and Erbring 2005, Sunstein 2009), where there is a fear that public discourse in the United States will be reduced to a space where "We don't know, can't understand and can barely conceive of 'those people' who live just a few miles away" (Bishop 2008, p. 114).

Through a differential exposure of information, there arises the potential for severe levels of animosity toward those who do not have a space in their own personalized community and discursive sphere. In "The Outrage Industry," Jeffrey Berry and Sarah Sobieraj (2014) identify a multitude of ways in which partisan media outlets evoke strong negative emotions about political opponents, often times at a very personal level, largely to reinforce group boundaries. These sentiments are not just limited to views of the parties and their policy proposals; they have a personal element as well. As an example, the Pew Research Center found that when Republicans and Democrats were asked to rate each other on a 0–100 "thermometer," both groups gave very low ratings to the people in the opposing party. Democrats give Republicans a mean rating of 31, while Republicans give Democrats a mean rating of only 29, while noting "a growing contempt that many Republicans and Democrats have for the opposing party"(Pew Research Center, 2016) This hostility is purposely infused into partisan news sources (online or offline) in an effort to develop a deep personal connection to the audience member, and increase the likelihood of the user returning to the news source in the future (Berry and Sobieraj 2014).

In recent years, the Pew Research Center has identified a large amount of empirical evidence that seems to confirm this rise of animosity among political partisans in the United States. For example, a national survey indicated found that among those who identify themselves as being highly engaged in politics, 70 percent of Democrats and 62 percent of Republicans say they are "afraid of the other party" (Pew Research, June 22, 2016). A major element of partisan polarization "has been the growing contempt that many Republicans and Democrats have for the opposing party" (Pew Research Center, 2016). Today, negative feelings about the opposing party are as powerful—and in many cases more powerful—as are positive feelings about one's own party. Nearly half of Republicans and Democrats (44 percent each) say they "almost never" agree with the other party's positions (Pew Research, 2016).

For Democrats, no single critique resonates more than the notion that Republicans are closed-minded. The Pew Research Center (2016) found that 70 percent of Democrats believe that Republicans are more closed-minded than other Americans, and nearly as many Democrats (67 percent) say the people in their party are more open-minded than other

Americans. In this national survey, Pew (2016) also found that 42 percent of Democrats believe that Republicans are more dishonest than other Americans, 35 percent say they are more immoral, and 33 percent say they are more unintelligent. Among Democrats, highly negative views of the GOP have followed a rising trajectory—from 37 percent in 2008 up to 43 percent in 2014 and rising to 55 percent during the summer of 2016.

Many Republicans also seem to think that Democrats fall short on several important personal traits as well. While more than half of Republicans (52 percent) view Democrats as more closed-minded than other Americans, nearly as many say Democrats are more immoral (47 percent), lazier (46 percent) and more dishonest (45 percent). Not only do almost half of Republicans say Democrats are lazier than other Americans, 59 percent also say that the members of their own party are more hard-working. Likewise, half of Republicans view themselves as more moral than other Americans (Pew Research, 2016). Today, 58 percent of Republicans have a very unfavorable impression of the Democratic Party, up from 46 percent in 2014 and just 32 percent during the 2008 election year (Pew Research Center, 2016), while an earlier 2014 Pew Research national survey found that 66 percent of "consistently conservative" Republicans think that Democrat party policies threaten the nation's well-being.

What is also noteworthy is that the rise in hostilities has correlated positively with the diffusion of Internet technology into the everyday lives of Americans. In 1994, not exactly a time defined by warm partisan relations, a majority of Republicans had unfavorable impressions of the Democratic Party, but just 17 percent had *very* unfavorable opinions. Similarly, while most Democrats viewed the GOP unfavorably, just 16 percent had a very unfavorable views. Since then, highly negative views have more than doubled: 43 percent of Republicans and 38 percent of Democrats now view the opposite party in strongly negative terms. In sum, partisan animosity has increased substantially between 1994 and 2014. In each party, the percentage of those with a highly negative attitude toward the opposing party has more than doubled since 1994. Today, a high amount of intense partisans believe that the opposing party's policies "are so misguided that they threaten the nation's well-being" (Pew Research Center, 2014).

A handful of research questions arise based upon this body of literature. First, do partisans still engage in patterns of selective news exposure, and, if so, what venues do they commonly attend? While it seems likely that political news seekers still utilize this practice, this research project aims to identify which sources correlate to political partisanship, and how strong are those relationships? Second, will the data replicate the Pew Research Center's findings regarding partisanship and the negative emotional states (specifically, feelings of antipathy and perception of blame for societal conditions) toward political opponents? Third, is there a significantly higher amount of outgroup-based antipathy for partisans who engage in high levels of selective exposure with those who do not? Finally, will the data show that blame toward opposing political groups can be differentiated between those partisans who engage in high levels of selective exposure to political news?

What is expected is that partisans will engage in higher levels of selective exposure, and will hold higher levels of antipathy and blame toward political opponents. This is explained by constant reinforcement leading to attitudinal extremity in patterns identified by earlier research. However, there is relatively fewer within-group comparisons among the most committed supporters of political parties. Is it fair to say that those who are partisan and engage in high levels of selective exposure take a qualitatively different tone toward opposition than other group members that seemingly are observing a greater variety of political information?

**Hypotheses**

Based on a review of the literature, four predictions have been formed.

1 The stronger someone identifies themselves with a political party, the more likely they engage in higher levels of selective exposure on political news.
2 Partisans, whether Democrat or Republican, will hold higher levels of antipathy and blame toward political opponents
3 Partisans engaging in selective exposure patterns will exhibit higher levels of personal antipathy toward political opponents than other Partisans.
4 Partisans engaging in selective exposure patterns will be more likely to blame the country's problems on political opposition.

**Methodology**

To test these hypotheses, an online sample of 398 US adults conducted during the 2016 Presidential Election season. Minor financial incentives to induce survey responses, which resulted in a fairly strong response

Table 1. Demographics of Online Survey Sample

| Age (Mean = 44.48) | Percent | Racial Identity | Percent | Gender | Percent | Educational Attainment | Percent |
|---|---|---|---|---|---|---|---|
| 18–25 | 18.4 | White | 69.8 | Male | 47.7 | Masters or PhD | 11.0 |
| 26–35 | 19.6 | Black | 12.3 | Female | 52.3 | 4-year College | 26.6 |
| 36–45 | 14.6 | Hispanic | 8.8 | | | Some College | 39.2 |
| 46–55 | 14.7 | Asian American | 2.5 | | | HS Degree | 19.6 |
| 56–65 | 18.6 | Mixed or Other | 6.5 | | | Less than HS Degree | 2.8 |
| Over 65 | 14.1 | | | | | | |

rate of 82.6 percent. Additionally, this survey relied on a sampling frame that roughly matched the US population in terms of age, race, gender, and education. The following table indicates the demographics of those in the sample. In sum, the sample represents a wide age range. Sample racial statistics are fairly approximate to the US population, with a slight oversampling of white Americans and underrepresentation of Hispanics and Asian Americans, also with a slight oversampling of women and those who have higher levels of educational attainment (Table 1).

Items used in the survey often relied on asking the respondent to self-identify their interests, attitudes, and behaviors. For example, Political Identity was measured by having the respondent choose between one of six categories, ranging from "consistently conservative" to "consistently liberal." The distribution of political identities of this sample can be seen in Table 2 below:

Table 2. Political Identities of Survey Respondents

| Political Identity of Respondent | N | Percentage of Respondents |
|---|---|---|
| Consistently Conservative | 62 | 15.6 |
| Mostly Conservative | 84 | 21.1 |
| Mixed, but leaning Conservative | 101 | 25.4 |
| Mixed, but learning Liberal | 55 | 13.8 |
| Mostly Liberal | 59 | 14.8 |
| Consistently Liberal | 37 | 9.3 |
| TOTALS | 398 | 100.0 |

Measuring selective exposure to news relied on having the respondent tell us how much they actively seek news from a menu of potential news sources. The list of news sources included the following items: Listening to NPR, Viewing the Rush Limbaugh Show, The O'Reilly Factor, Real Time with Bill Maher, The Rachel Maddow Show, Reading the Wall Street Journal (paper or online), Reading the New York Times (paper or online), Watching on TV or online browsing CNN, PBS, MSNBC and Fox News, or "liking" a political party or figure (Democrat or Republican), and Liking a Political Pundit (Liberal or Conservative). Among each of these news sources, respondents could self-report if they are viewed "always," "regularly," "sometimes," "rarely," or "never."

These measures of self-reported news viewing were then correlated with political identity to determine which source(s) were significantly more likely to be preferred by conservatives or liberals. Table 3 indicates which news sources were significantly correlated to political identity:

Table 3. Correlations between Political Identity and News Sources

| News Source | Preferred by Conservatives | No Significant Correlation to Political Identity | Preferred by Liberals |
|---|---|---|---|
| Listening to NPR | | .028 | |
| Rush Limbaugh | .328** | | |
| Bill O'Reilly | .301** | | |
| Bill Maher | | .010 | |
| Rachel Maddow | | .041 | |
| Wall Street Journal | .194** | | |
| New York Times | | .068 | |
| CNN | | .079 | |
| PBS | | .091 | |
| MSNBC | | .041 | |
| Fox News | .318** | | |
| Liking a GOP Politician or Party on Facebook | .189** | | |
| Like a GOP Pundit on Facebook | .208** | | |
| Liking Democrat Politician or Party on Facebook | | | .179** |
| Like a Liberal Pundit on Facebook | | | .238** |

**. Significant at a 99 percent confidence level.

Table 4. Measuring Antipathy and Blame toward Political Opposition

| Antipathy (5 items used) | Blame (5 items used) |
|---|---|
| People who support (liberals/conservatives) are not real Americans | (liberals/conservatives) are the biggest problem that the country faced today |
| I prefer to live near people who share my political viewpoints | The ideas of (liberals/conservatives) are a threat to the well-being of this country |
| I have no interest in forming close relationships with (liberals/conservatives) | The policies of (liberals/conservatives) nearly always result in severe damage to this country |
| (liberals/conservatives) are usually ignorant people | (liberals/conservatives) have no good political ideas at all |
| (liberals/conservatives) have low moral character | (liberals/conservatives) are largely responsible for the high levels of conflict in our political climate |
| Cronbach's Alpha (Conservatives) = .916 | Cronbach's Alpha (Conservatives) = .952 |
| Cronbach's Alpha (Liberals) = .870 | Cronbach's Alpha (Liberals) = .951 |

Then, in order to measure "selective exposure," each conservative had their total viewing of the sources that correlated with political conservatism (Rush Limbaugh, Bill O'Reilly, Wall Street Journal, Fox News, Liking Politicians and Political Pundits on Facebook) summed together and then divided by all news viewing that they engaged in. This gave each respondent a GOP selective exposure score that ranged from 0 (no selectivity) to 100 (fully partisan selectivity). This same process was used for those who identified as liberals, where those who received all of their news from following liberal news sources on Facebook would receive a score of 100, and those who showed a wider selection on news sources would have scores closer to 0.

The dependent variables of "Antipathy" and "Blame" relied on indexes that each contained five questions. These indexes were found to have a high degree of internal reliability according to Cronbach's Alpha, a statistic that measures the consistency of responses among multiple questions attempting to measure an underlying concept. This items used to form these indexes can be seen in Table 4. The online survey first asked whether the respondent to identify as liberal or conservative (as discussed above), then asked the respondent about their beliefs toward people who were among the political opposition. Each item was scored on a 0-10 feeling thermometer (0 = Fully Disagree to 10 = Fully Agree) and summed together so that each respondent had scores for antipathy and blame that ranged from scores of 0 to 50.

**Results**

Testing hypothesis one involved conducting a one-way Analysis of Variance (ANOVA) test to see if the mean scores between these six different political identity groups show any significant differences in value regarding selective exposure levels. The data show that people who define themselves as consistently aligned to a political party (whether they were Democrat or Republican) were more likely to engage in higher rates of selective exposure. In Table 5, we can see that the selective exposure score to conservative news sites increases the more someone defines themselves as being consistently conservative ($F = 18.577$, P-value $<.001$). What can be seen is that the average selective exposure scores for "consistently conservative" had a mean score ranging from 40.48 to 52.39, while "Mostly Conservative" respondents also engage in significantly higher selectivity rates of viewing conservative news sites than do others. It can also be seen that the mean scores for consistently conservative (46.43) and mostly conservative (45.38) are substantially higher than the mean scores of consistently liberal (15.79) and mostly liberal (22.86), a pattern consistent with the prediction made in hypothesis one.

Likewise, a similar pattern can be found among Democrats. In Table 6, the selective exposure rates to liberal news sites were highest for those who were consistently liberal (42.85), followed by those who are mostly liberal (29.62). In contrast, the consistently conservative (20.75) and mostly conservative (10.00) showed notably less interest in attending to liberal sites.

Table 5. Selective Exposure Rates and Conservative News Sites

|  | N | Mean | Std Error | Confidence Lower Bound | Confidence Upper Bound |
|---|---|---|---|---|---|
| Consistently Conservative | 51 | 46.43 | 2.96 | 40.48 | 52.39 |
| Mostly Conservative | 70 | 45.38 | 2.59 | 40.19 | 50.56 |
| Leaning Conservative | 80 | 29.76 | 1.72 | 26.33 | 33.18 |
| Leaning Liberal | 34 | 31.34 | 3.26 | 24.70 | 37.98 |
| Mostly Liberal | 48 | 22.86 | 2.31 | 18.21 | 27.51 |
| Consistently Liberal | 25 | 15.79 | 3.89 | 7.74 | 23.83 |
| Total | 308 | 34.03 | 1.21 | 31.64 | 36.43 |

Table 6. Selective Exposure Rates and Liberal News Sites

| | N | Mean | Std Error | Confidence Lower Bound | Confidence Upper Bound |
|---|---|---|---|---|---|
| Consistently Conservative | 53 | 20.75 | 5.62 | 9.46 | 32.04 |
| Mostly Conservative | 70 | 10.00 | 3.61 | 2.79 | 17.20 |
| Leaning Conservative | 83 | 19.27 | 4.35 | 10.61 | 27.94 |
| Leaning Liberal | 37 | 27.02 | 7.40 | 12.01 | 42.03 |
| Mostly Liberal | 49 | 29.62 | 7.14 | 11.22 | 48.03 |
| Consistently Liberal | 27 | 42.85 | 8.95 | 28.49 | 57.21 |
| Total | 319 | 22.88 | 2.35 | 18.24 | 27.51 |

Overall, Tables 5 and 6 confirm hypothesis one: the more one defines themselves as being affiliated with a political party, the more they will engage in selective exposure to news sources. This pattern is a bit easier to see among conservatives, where there is more observable significant correlation between available news sources and political identity. To my surprise, liberal political identity did not significantly correlate to nearly as many news sources, which led to perhaps a less reliable measure of liberal selective exposure than I had expected. I will revisit this idea later in the discussion section.

To conduct a test of hypothesis two, it was necessary to collapse the political identity categories to four groups: consistently/mostly conservative, leaning conservative, leaning liberal, and consistently/mostly liberal. The aim is to conduct a two-group mean comparison t-test of antipathy and blame which compares those who lean toward one party versus those who appear to be more firmly committed to their partisanship.

Beginning with conservatives, it can be seen in Table 7 that levels of antipathy for liberals are higher among those who are consistently conservative (T = 3.579, P = .001), where there is a significantly higher antipathy score (24.21). Those who are more committed to conservatism do seem to hold more hostility than do others. A similar pattern was also found with regards to blame. Table 8 shows that the average amount of blame for current political conditions and climate is significantly higher (T = 5.609, P < .001) for those who hold a stronger group affiliation to conservative politics (a score of 29.36 versus only 18.05 for those who lean conservative)

While a patterns of antipathy and blame holds among conservatives, testing hypothesis two also requires comparing the opinions among

Table 7. Antipathy for Liberals by Conservatives

|  | N | Mean | Std. Error |
|---|---|---|---|
| Consistently/Mostly Conservative | 122 | 24.21 | 1.35 |
| Leaning Conservative | 83 | 17.37 | 1.35 |

Table 8. Blame of Liberals by Conservatives

|  | N | Mean | Std. Error |
|---|---|---|---|
| Consistently/Mostly Conservative | 123 | 29.36 | 1.53 |
| Leaning Conservative | 79 | 18.05 | 1.31 |

liberals as well. These two-group comparisons were made in Tables 9 and 10. With regards to antipathy, it has been found that the mostly/consistently liberal do hold significantly higher levels (T = 2.676, P = .009) of hostile feelings toward conservatives (20.20 versus 14.64). Likewise, significantly higher levels of blame toward conservatives (T = 3.008, P = .003) was also found among the more committed liberals. Taken together, Table 7 through ten indicate empirical support for hypothesis two.

Conducting a test of hypothesis three involved comparing mean scores of antipathy held toward members of the opposing political party. In order to conduct this test, the variable of selective news exposure was categorized so that any score above 50 was recoded as engaging in high levels of selectivity. This allowed for a two-group comparison (for conservatives and liberals) with the antipathy scores of those engaging in above-average amounts of selectivity could be compared to other party members who had a wider news exposure pattern.

Table 9. Antipathy of Conservatives by Liberals

|  | N | Mean | Std. Error |
|---|---|---|---|
| Consistently/Mostly Liberal | 84 | 20.20 | 1.36 |
| Leaning Liberal | 51 | 14.64 | 1.56 |

Table 10. Blame of Conservatives by Liberals

|  | N | Mean | Std. Error |
|---|---|---|---|
| Consistently/Mostly Liberal | 81 | 26.58 | 1.56 |
| Leaning Liberal | 47 | 18.61 | 2.13 |

Table 11. Antipathy of Liberals and Selective Exposure among Conservatives

|  | N | Mean | Std. Error |
|---|---|---|---|
| Conservatives, High Selectivity Level | 35 | 20.97 | 2.26 |
| Conservatives, Low Selectivity Levels | 87 | 25.51 | 1.64 |

Table 12. Liberals, Selective Exposure, and Antipathy held toward Conservatives

|  | N | Mean | Std. Error |
|---|---|---|---|
| Liberals, High Selectivity Level | 26 | 22.84 | 2.35 |
| Liberals, Low Selectivity Levels | 58 | 19.01 | 1.66 |

Table 11 shows the results of a two-group mean comparison t-test for conservatives and their levels of antipathy held toward liberals. It was found that there were no significant differences in the mean scores of conservatives who engaged in higher levels of selective exposure versus those who did not (T = -1.621, P-value = .109). Surprisingly, the highly selective actually showed a little less antipathy, according to the data.

Similarly, liberals who were highly selective also did not show increased levels of antipathy toward political opponents. Table 12 shows that there are no significant differences in the mean scores of antipathy between these two groups (T = 1.329, P-value = .190). Tables 11 and 12, taken together, show that there is no empirical support for hypothesis three. Partisans who engage in high levels of selective exposure do not appear to show significantly more antipathy toward political opponents than do other partisans that engage in a greater variety of political news consumption.

Finally, hypothesis four tests whether partisans engaging in selective exposure patterns will be more likely to blame the country's problems on political opposition. This again involves a two-group mean comparison t-test for conservatives and the amount of blame that they held toward liberals, comparing the highly selective versus others that are strongly partisan. Table 13 shows that there is virtually no difference at all in the opinions of these two groups (T = 0.22, P-value = .983), with a mean score of 29.41 among the highly selective, and 29.34 among the other conservatives in this sample.

Likewise, the data shown in Table 14 indicates that the opinions of highly selective liberals (mean score of 28.84) did not significantly differ from other members of their party (T = 1.042, P-value = .302). It does not

Table 13. Conservatives, Selective Exposure, and blame for the nation's problems

|  | N | Mean | Std. Error |
|---|---|---|---|
| Conservatives, High Selectivity Level | 34 | 29.41 | 2.41 |
| Conservatives, Low Selectivity Levels | 89 | 29.34 | 1.56 |

Table 14. Liberals, Selective Exposure, and blame for the nation's problems

|  | N | Mean | Std. Error |
|---|---|---|---|
| Liberals, High Selectivity Level | 26 | 28.84 | 2.52 |
| Liberals, Low Selectivity Levels | 55 | 25.50 | 1.97 |

appear that pursuing a pattern of selective exposure for political partisans leads to any excessive levels of blame for the state of the nation, which seems to be true for both conservatives and liberals. Overall, the data do not show support for hypothesis four.

**Discussion and conclusion**

To summarize the results about, three main points can be identified. First, the data show that the stronger one holds their political affiliation, whether Republican or Democrat, the more likely they will engage in a pattern of news preference that seemingly reinforces viewpoints. By analyzing various news sources with political identification, there seems to be a clearer pattern of selective exposure among conservatives than liberals, at least in this data set. Fairly strong correlations were found among Republicans with platforms such as Fox News, Rush Limbaugh, the Wall Street Journal, and other sources that have been previously recognized as being more appealing to conservatives (Berry and Sobieraj 2014, Gross 2015; Pew Research Center, 2014). However, in an unexpected finding, liberal identification did not correlate significantly to any traditional mass media news organization. Instead, those on the political left seem geared to a preference for following their party, favorite politicians, and political pundits directly through social media—on platforms where there is little narration or gatekeeping by news organizations. It appears possible that selective exposure patterns among conservatives and liberals take on noticeably different paths than others have observed, with liberals having more of a preference for direct "non-news" sources to receive political information. Unfortunately, answering this question could not be achieved with the data currently available.

Second, perhaps unsurprisingly, political partisanship significantly and positively correlates to polarized attitudes toward members of the opposition party. Overall, 242 of 398 respondents (60.8 percent) in this sample indicated a clear preference for one political party, with many of those people showing distressingly high levels of animosity for their fellow citizens. It is not difficult to see how these feelings currently characterize the highly confrontational political climate in the United States, where attitudinal extremity reigns over a large percent of the populous. Moreover, data from the Pew Research Center (2014) have shown that liberals and conservatives have both increasingly defined politics as a zero-sum game, defining an optimal political outcome in terms of winning and losing, rather than on finding compromise. With this working definition of successful politics, the idea of finding consensus based on a careful deliberation of various assumptions and viewpoints seems highly unlikely.

What is more complicated is attempting to identify how this climate can be altered by changes in the way citizens receive news and attend to information in the public sphere. This brings us to the third main finding of this research project: when controlling for the strength of political identity, attending to more diverse sources of information does not seem to reduce hostility toward other citizens. Among both the political left and right, strongly committed political supporters that engage in relatively lower amounts of partisan-based selective exposure have attitudes that are virtually indistinguishable for those "living in the bubble" of continual reinforcement. Results like this are troubling for those who believe that a more self-aware commitment to seeking out various viewpoints will increase ambiguity and decrease animosity among the general public. Instead, it appears possible that many who are strongly partisan may have passed a "point of no return" regarding American politics. While social scientists would like to believe that having liberals listen to the Rush Limbaugh show while conservatives follow Rachel Maddow online could increase ambiguity and polarization, the data here cannot support this potential outcome.

Another concern related to public discourse, attitudinal extremity and the role of media has been the recent phenomenon of "fake news" sites that seem to thrive on the Internet, especially through social networking site newsfeeds (Bauder 2017). Previous research on this topic has long conceded that partisan-based selective exposure entails a biased exposure to information and alters political thoughts and actions. However, less attention has been paid to how effectively false information is persuasive, how quickly it spreads among homogenous groups, and how it contributes to anger and perceptions of attitudinal certainty. Since the 2016 US Presidential election, this has drawn interest from political activist groups and educators (Najmabadi 2016, Stanley 2016), and will likely receive a lot of interest from social scientists.

While it is possible that exposure to a greater variety of political facts and viewpoints will do little to change our current political climate, others have added that one of the "benefits" of increased polarization is its positive correlation to higher levels of political activity (Gainous and Wagner 2011, Levendusky 2013; Pew Research 2014, 2016). However, an increased citizen commitment to politics that is largely based upon anger, closed-mindedness, and an ignorance of political facts is hardly desirable for America's future. Perhaps just as perplexing to those who study media and political opinion is the realization that an expanded public sphere over the last 20 years has seemingly reduced ambiguity rather than having increased it. On one hand, the enormous expansion of mass and social media that has been observed in the twenty-first century has consistently found its way into the hands of hundreds of millions of political non-elites. This should have created a more enlightened public that engages in complex, reasoned discourse that is filled with nuance and uncertainty. Few would describe America's current political climate in those terms, where anger, blame and the superficiality of political attitudes appear to have grown. These news media technologies have seemingly created more of a political dystopia than utopia in the United State, despite the expansion of the public sphere occurring in a way that should have created a healthier Democracy.

In our current socio-political context, continual partisan reinforcement and personal motivations for attitudinal certainty act as a threat to ambiguity, potentially leading to higher levels of extremism. It is important for the public to realize that virtually all citizens interested in political issues while also having access to a wide array of mediums can make them susceptible to becoming more closed-minded and less able to appreciate differences in opinion. When people become more self-aware of these threats, then begin to avoid the patterns of reinforcement currently found in selective exposure and discourse, there will be hope for a more respectful, less toxic public sphere in the future.

## Works Cited

Adamic, Lada, and Natalie Glance, 2005, The Political Sphere and the 2004 Election: Divided they blog. *Proceedings of the 3rd international workshop on Link Discovery*, 36-43. http://dl.acm.org/citation.cfm?id=1134277. Accessed on May 16, 2017.

Bakshy, Eytan, Solomon Messing, and Lada Adamic, 2015, *Replication Data for: Exposure to Ideologically Diverse News and Opinion on Facebook*. https://doi.org/10.7910/dvn/ldj7ms Harvard Dataverse, V2. Accessed on May 18, 2017.

Bauder, David, 2017, January 18, "Study Illustrates Facebook's Growth as campaign news source", The Seattle Times. http://www.seattletimes.com/business/study-shows-facebooks-growth-as-campaign-news-source/. Accessed on May 14, 2017.

Bennett, W. Lance, and Shanto Iyengar, 2008, "A New Era of Minimal Effects? The Changing Foundations of Political Communication," Journal of Communication **58**(4), pp. 707–31.

Berry, Jeffrey M., and Sarah Sobieraj, 2014, The Outrage Industry, Oxford, UK: Oxford University Press.

Bishop, Ben, 2008, The Big Sort, New York, NY: Houghton Mifflin Company.

Festinger, Leon, 1957, A Theory of Cognitive Dissonance, Stanford, CA: Stanford University Press.

Dahlberg, Lincoln, 2007, "Rethinking the Fragmentation of the Cyberpublic: From Consensus to Contestation," New Media and Society **9**(5), pp. 827–47.

Freedman, Jonathan L., and David O. Sears, 1965, "Selective Exposure," in L. Berkowitz, ed., Advances in Experimental Social Psychology II, New York, NY: Academic Press, pp. 57–97.

Gainous, Jason, and Kevin Wagner, 2011, Rebooting American Politics: The Internet Revolution, New York, NY: Rowman & Littlefield.

Galston, William A., 2004, "The Impact of the Internet on Civic Life: An Early Assessment," in V.V. Gehring, ed., The Internet in public life, Oxford, UK: Rowman and Littlefield, pp. 59–78.

Galston, William A., 2005, "The Internet Fosters More Divisiveness in Politics," in J.D. Torr, ed., The Internet: Opposing Viewpoints, Farmington Hills, MI: Greenhaven Press, pp. 47–57.

Gross, Benjamin, 2015, "What Makes Someone a Cyber Balkan? Finding the Linkages between Social Psychology and Self-Selectivity in US Politics Online," Atlantic Journal of Communication **23**(4), pp. 225–36.

Habermas, Jurgen, 1989, The Structural Transformation of the Public Sphere: An Inquiry into a Category of Bourgeois Society, Cambridge, UK: Polity Press.

Herrmann, John, 2016, August 24, "Inside Facebook's (Totally Insane, Unintentionally Gigantic, Hyperpartisan) Political-Media Machine". *New York Times Magazine*, Page MM 50. https://www.nytimes.com/2016/08/28/magazine/inside-facebooks-totally-insane-unintentionally-gigantic-hyperpartisan-political-media-machine.html?smid=fb-nytimes&smtyp=cur Accessed on May 4, 2017.

Hogg, Michael A., 1992, The Social Psychology of Group Cohesiveness, New York, NY: New York University Press.

Iyengar, Shanto, and Kyu S. Hahn, 2009, "Red Media, Blue Media: Evidence of Ideological Selectivity in Media Use," Journal of Communication **59**(1), pp. 19–39.

Katz, James E., and Ronald E. Rice, 2002, Social Consequences of Internet Use: Access, Involvement, and Interaction, Boston: MIT Press.

Keegan, John, 2016, May 18, "Blue Feed, Red Feed". *Wall Street Journal*. http://graphics.wsj.com/blue-feed-red-feed/#/sterling-castile. Accessed on May 16, 2017.

Klapper, Joseph, 1960, The Effects of Mass Communication, New York, NY: Free Press.

Levendusky, Matthew, 2013, How Partisan Media Polarize America, Chicago: University of Chicago Press.

Manjoo, Farhad, 2008, True Enough: Learning to Live in a Post-Fact Society, Hoboken, NJ: John Wiley & Sons, Inc.

Myers, David G., and Helmut Lamm, 1976, "The Group Polarization Phenomenon," Psychological Bulletin **83**(4), pp. 602–27.

Najmabadi, Shannon, 2016, December 12, "How Can Students Be Taught to Detect Fake News and Dubious Claims?" *Chronicle of Higher Education*.

Nie, Norman H., and Lutz Erbring, 2005, "Internet Use Decreases Social Interaction," in J.D. Torr, ed., The Internet: Opposing Viewpoints, Farmington Hills, MI: Greenhaven Press, pp. 28–34.

Pew Research Center, 2014, June 12, Political Polarization in the American Public, Washington, DC: Pew Research Center.

Pew Research Center, 2016, June 22, Partisanship and Political Animosity in 2016, Washington, DC: Pew Research Center.

Putnam, Robert D., 2000, Bowling Alone: The Collapse and Revival of American Community, New York, NY: Simon and Schuster.

Stanley, Jay, 2016, December 12, "Fixing Fake News". *American Civil Liberties Union*. https://www.aclu.org/blog/free-future/fixing-fake-news. Accessed on April 16, 2017.

Stroud, Naomi J., 2011, Niche News: The Politics of News Choice, Oxford, UK: Oxford University Press.

Sunstein, Cass R., 2007, Republic.com 2.0: Revenge of the Blogs, Princeton, NJ: Princeton University Press.

Sunstein, Cass R., 2009, Going to Extremes: How Like Minds Unite and Divide, Oxford, UK: Oxford University Press.

Tufecki, Zeynep, 2016, May 19, "The Real Bias Built in at Facebook" *New York Times*. Page A27. https://www.nytimes.com/2016/05/19/opinion/the-real-bias-built-in-at-facebook.html. Accessed on May 18, 2017.

Vacker, Barry, 2000, "Global Village or World Bazaar?," in A.B. Albarran, and D.H. Goff, eds., Understanding the Web: Social, Political, and Economic Dimensions of the Internet, Ames, IA: Iowa State University Press, pp. 211–38.

Van Alstyne, Marshall., and Erik Brynjolfsson, 1996, Electronic Communities: Global Village or Cyberbalkans?, Boston: Sloan School, MIT.

Wachbroit, Robert, 2004, "Reliance and Reliability: The Problem of Information on the Internet," in V.V. Gehring, ed., The Internet in public life, Oxford, UK: Rowman & Littlefield, pp. 29–41.

# BOOK

## WHY THE WENDE?

*How a Forbidden Religion Swept the World.* By Bart D. Ehrman, New York, NY: Simon & Schuster, 2018. $28.

Germans like to talk about the "Constantinian shift" (*die konstantinische Wende*) that began in 312 with the conversion of the emperor and the subsequent (313) "Edict of Milan," which granted full religious tolerance to Christians (and others), and that culminated in Theodosius I's banning paganism and establishing Christianity as the state religion (381–392). At the time of Jesus' death, experts guess, there may have been twenty or so Christians. By the year 400 that number had soared to something like 30,000,000, or half the population of the Roman empire. A "shift" for the ages, evidently.

But why did it happen and what did it mean? If all human actions, as Freud said of dreams, are overdetermined, precisely explaining the personal and social processes that shaped the choice of so many myriads will be impossible. One might as well begin by looking to Edward Gibbon. Ehrman first naively claims that Gibbon "conceded that ultimate success derived from its (Christianity's) spiritual superiority and God's personal oversight"; but he quickly admits that the great historian meant no such thing: the key to such rapid growth lay in five "secondary causes", which Ehrman acknowledges and expands on. Meanwhile, he agrees with Gibbon in limiting himself to non-supernatural agencies.

1 "The inflexible, and ... intolerant zeal of Christians." Ehrman's term for this is "exclusivity." Pagan religions were famously accepting of other cults, had no notion of heresy, seldom engaged in persecution, and then only when the Roman authorities feared a threat to the well-being of the state. Christian faith was an all-or-nothing proposition (despite some sturdy vestiges of syncretism); and, once the hierarchy acquired judicial power, it could severely punish all deviations from orthodoxy. Ehrman might have mentioned the landmark figure of Priscillian, the Spanish bishop, who was executed in 385 for promoting a version of Manichaeism.

2 The doctrine of immortality. Pagans generally had no belief in life after death; so the prospect of a blissful eternity must have been a powerful influence on them, especially if E.R. Dodds and others were right to argue that by the fourth century paganism had fallen into "weakness and weariness." Ehrman adds to this the negative factor of fear of hell. Lucretius (died *c.* 55 BCE) may have mocked the fanciful terrors of Hades; but the New Testament made a strong case for divine vengeance.

3 Miracles. Ehrman, who went from a devout evangelical graduate of the Moody Bible Institute and Wheaton College to an agnostic professor of Religious Studies at U.N.C., Chapel

Hill, and the popular author of many demythologizing books about Christianity and Scripture, stresses that the miracles attributed to the apostles and early Christian saints might not have actually happened (he won't call them fabrications). But people *believed* they happened; and they told their friends and neighbors, and a mighty legend was launched. Stories of martyrdom too must have spread far and wide. Ehrman in fact cites simple word of mouth as a major engine of conversion that may have been as effective as preaching.

4 Strict Christian morality. There were only casual links between paganism and ethical behavior. Sacrifices mollified the Greek and Roman gods; and, ideally won their favor. But accounts of the gods' activities seldom made them out to be more upright than humans. Nonetheless, Zeus sometimes morphed into a henotheistic moral ruler—and people who believed in such a deity would be one step closer to the God of the Bible. (When it came to moral guidance, Ehrman says, the ancients turned to philosophy.) In any case, to the extent that they lived up, even partly, to Jesus' stringent code and formed high-minded communities, Christians may have set an appealing example to outsiders. Tertullian famously maintained that the pagans themselves were awed by the way Jesus' followers loved, and were ready to die for, one another (*Apologeticus pro Christianis*, 39). But, since the near-totality of converts left no written records behind, Ehrman doesn't press this point.

5 Strong ecclesiastical organization. Pagan religions had priests, but (practically) no sacred texts, no defined dogma, no *churches*. Religion was just a normal part of civic life and, for the most part, a local affair. Gods and divinized heroes were associated with particular regions, names, myths, and rites, as opposed to "Jesus Christ the same yesterday and today and forever" (Heb. 13.8). They had no genius like St. Paul, who systematized doctrine, tirelessly proselytized, founded numerous faith communities, kept in frequent touch with them, and traveled thousands of miles in so doing. Those communities provided not just a sense of belonging, but practical charity and help in time of need. Finally, Christianity laid a much lighter burden on converts than Judaism (which welcomed, though it didn't seek them out): no circumcision, no *kashrut*, no long, elaborate Torah, no Hebrew language.

Oddly, Ehrman doesn't discuss the liberating potential of Paul's teaching on justification. Again, this is a feature that can't be quantified; but we know from the Reformation and the First and Second Great Awakening in America what enormous psychological relief guilt-ridden believers can find in "amazing grace." Why shouldn't that have been available both before and after the "shift"? (Ehrman speculates that mass conversion to Christianity would have occurred even without Constantine.) And wasn't the potent sense of identification with Jesus-as-Savior a headier brew than the dutiful carrying out of ritual obligations to gods whom one could not "contact" in any subjective fashion, save perhaps for practitioners of mystery religions such as Mithraism?

But still, how did the shift happen so fast? Ehrman has no magic formula to apply to all the demographic evidence he's assembled here, just math. He reminds us that, just as with the exponential curve of compound interest, a continuous annual increase of less than 3 percent in the fourth century could raise the number of Christians from ca. three million to the thirty million cited above. In addition, if the person converted were the head of a household, then presumably his wife, children, and servants/slaves would convert as well.

The "triumph," then, in Ehrman's title is purely factual, like the final score of a game. Ehrman himself is no triumphalist. He sounds nostalgic when he reviews the countless easy-going, ideologically promiscuous pagan cults wiped out or driven underground by Christianity's dominance. Who knows how much may have been lost in their disappearance? Ehrman hints at but (wisely?) doesn't try to answer that question.

Given his position as a pilgrim from literal faith to modernity, one would have liked to see Ehrman tackle the polar opposite of his basically benign approach—the sort of vehement rejection of the "shift" that Nietzsche gives voice to The Anti-Christ 59 (1895):

> The whole work of the ancient world in vain: I have no words to express how I feel about something so monstrous.

And considering that this work was just preparatory, that the foundation for a labor to last millennia had just been laid with granite-like self-consciousness, the whole meaning of antiquity was in vain. What good are Greeks? What good are Romans?—All the prerequisites for a learned culture, all scientific methods were already there. The great, the incomparable art of reading well had already been discovered—that *sine qua non* for the handing down of culture, for the unity of knowledge; natural science linked to mathematics and mechanics, had set out on the very best path. A sense for facts, the last and most valuable of all the senses, had its schools, its tradition, which was already centuries old—is that understood?

Everything essential for getting to work had been found. The methods (this has to be said ten times over) are the essential thing, as well as the most difficult, and also the thing that has had for the longest time to contend with old habits and laziness. What we today, with unspeakable self-mastery—because we still have the bad instincts, the Christian ones, in our body—have won back: the free glance at the face of reality, the careful hand, the patience and seriousness in the finest details, the honesty of insight—it was already there! And it had been there for more than two thousand years. . . . Overnight no more than a memory: Greeks! Romans!

Well, Professor Nietzsche, the invalided classicist and fervent anti-theist, is a highly biased witness; and even though a cost-benefit analysis of the "shift" lies beyond Ehrman's scope here, his last two chapters, "Conversions and Coercions" and "Gains and Losses" do venture into the negative. He mourns the destruction of the Serapeum in Alexandria (391) and the notorious murder of the philosopher Hypatia (415), citing them as horrific markers of growing Christian intolerance, along with anti-Judaism. He takes time-out to deride the forged Donation of Constantine. Pagan religion was bound to lose the contest with Christianity; but did it have to be so violently repressed? It might be noted in passing that Robin Lane Fox's *Pagans and Christians* (1987) called attention to a larger-scale survival of pagan religious practice than Ehrman allows for. Ehrman sums up his case by maintaining that the Christianization of the Empire wasn't inevitable. "I do not celebrate it as a victory for the human race and a sign of cultural progress ... or a major sociopolitical set-back and cultural disaster."

But if the latter is true, why does he conclude by taking a sentimental journey to the Parthenon and wondering what might have been if Julian the Apostate had enjoyed a longer reign? Throughout the book Ehrman repeatedly calls himself a historian, i.e., a recorder, not a judge. But he plainly prefers Constantine's policy to Theodosius', and he grieves over the seemingly endless furor unleashed by the Christian obsession with "right belief." To the extent that he himself ever suffered from it, he's long since gotten over it. And the implicit question at the heart of his irenic, even-handed book is: why couldn't everybody else?

—*Peter Heinegg*

# BOOK

## THE ROAD TO MONOTHEISM

*The Exodus: How it Happened and Why it Matters.* By Richard Elliott Friedman, New York, NY: Harper One, 2017. xiv + 282 pp. $27.99.

Professor Richard Elliott Friedman (Jewish Studies, U. of Georgia, after 22 years at U.C., San Diego) has made a successful career out of combining solid biblical scholarship (much of it centered around the Documentary Hypothesis) with bold speculation. His lively, accessible style has won him many readers; and it's hard to come away from his books without being intellectually stimulated, though not necessarily convinced. What is one to make of his comparing the "Big Bang" to the cabalistic "shattering of God's unity," as presented in *The Disappearance of God* (1995)?

Newcomers to Friedman may be at least initially disappointed because he doesn't actually explain "how the Exodus happened." The whole account is so saturated with myth (e.g., the plagues and the claim the Israelites had an army of 600,000 men, cf. Ex. 12.37-38, Num. 1.46) that he quickly dismisses the great bulk of what is the Hebrew Bible's most important and dramatic event. This makes sense, since only fundamentalists could believe that, apart from all the preceding miracles, a horde of over two million people could survive for forty years in the wilderness of Sinai—without leaving a single archaeological trace behind. But, as well as skipping over all that narrative color, Friedman leaves some painful questions unasked. Why punish all of Egypt for the Pharaoh's divinely inflicted hardness of heart? Why did all the first-born, "from the first-born of Pharaoh, who sits upon his throne, even to the first-born of the maid-servant who is behind the mill" (Ex. 11:5) have to die? Was it the fault of all the conscripted grunts in the Egyptian cavalry (Ex. 14:26) that they were ordered to pursue the Israelites? And is it a problem that at Passover Jews to this day celebrate the death of the first-born Egyptians in the *Dayenu* song?

Friedman's thesis doesn't deal with any of this. He asserts that there *was* no massive Exodus. Only the Levites made the great crossing (the rest of Israel was composed of indigenous tribes in Canaan); and the Levites brought with them the worship of Yahweh, which fused with the Israelite cult of El and became the monotheistic faith of the Jews. Friedman presents many links in his argumentative chain, most of which are quite interesting and none of which is conclusive. (When all is said and done, the historical possibility remains that the entire tale of the Exodus, including the person of Moses, is fiction.)

Friedman does have a lot of suggestive bits to work with: (1) Of the eight Israelites with Egyptian names, all of them are Levites; (2) Both passages (Ex. 3:25, 6:2–3) revealing the name Yahweh cite Moses the Levite as the recipient, and both occur in Levite sources; (3)

The long (and, for most readers, utterly tedious) chapters on the Tabernacle (Ex. 25-30, 35-40) can be linked to the Egyptian tent of Ramses II; (4) The ark of the covenant is similar to Egyptian ritual boats; (5) All seven items of "Egyptian" lore in the Exodus story come from Levite sources; (6) All eleven references to circumcision in a legal context occur in Levitical sources, as do; (7) all texts about slavery during and after the time in Egypt. (The root of the word Levite means "attached," which Friedman sees as indicating the outsider status of the Levites, first as slaves in Egypt, then as a landless tribe in Israel.); (8) All fifty-two references to aliens are found in Levite sources; (9) All fifty-two references to the "sanctuary" (*miqdash*), which in the triumphal Song of the Sea chanted by Miriam in Ex. 15:1 b-18 is where "the people" enter, identify it as the Temple or Tabernacle, into which only the Levites are allowed. Friedman says all this is too much to be merely coincidental; and besides, why would *any* people trace their origins to the debased condition of slaves in a foreign country—unless it were true?

Many experts have stressed that, however many individuals entered Canaan from Sinai, they would have found a Hebrew-speaking native population that had long been there. This emerges from a vast amount of archaeological and linguistic materials. Friedman quotes Jeffrey Tigay (U. of Pennsylvania): "The names of more than 1,200 pre-exilic Israelites are known from Hebrew inscriptions and foreign inscriptions relating to Israel."

(And about half of them contain the word "Yahweh" in one form or another.) Among other things, this serves to refute the occasional Islamist claim that Israelis are foreign interlopers in Palestine.

Friedman doesn't know exactly when and how the Levites joined up with the rest of Israel (or what their life in Egypt was like). And what, if any, were the connections between Moses and Midian? Could Moses have been, not a refugee there, but a Midianite himself, like Zipporah and her family? Was Yahweh the god of Midian and is that why Moses was told to lead the people of Israel all the way to Mt. Sinai (in Midian)? Or is there anything to Freud's explosive theory that Moses was an Egyptian who got his monotheism from Pharaoh Akhenaten's? (No.) But there are many intriguing leads (e.g., Abraham had a son named Midian with his later wife Keturah) in this minimally documented territory; and Friedman has to admit that he can't get beyond conjecture.

In any case, the Levites eventually arrived in Israel, and Yahweh merged with El as the sole God of Israel. Many critics trace the completion of this process to the Babylonian exile (587–538 BCE), mostly notably to Second Isaiah (chapter 40–55); but Friedman insists that it took place much earlier. He quotes many texts to this effect, such as 2 Sam. 22:32/Ps. 18:32 ("For who is God, but the LORD? And who is a rock, except our God?"), possibly from late in David's reign (ca. 1,000–960), and Dt. 32: 39 ("I, even I, am he, and there is no god beside me"), which is written in archaic Hebrew (all translations RSV).

This sounds reasonable enough, but Friedman ignores the vast amount of evidence for the belief and practice of henotheism before the Exile. In both versions of the Ten Commandment (Ex. 20:2–17 and Dt. 5:6–21), the LORD condemns idolatry by saying that he is "a jealous God," but why be would he jealous of completely non-existent idols? (And what about the chilling proclamation of corporate guilt in "visiting the iniquity of the fathers upon the third and the fourth generation of those that hate me"?) The metaphor of God as the angry husband who chastises Israel, his faithless bride, for running after false gods, most vividly portrayed in Ezekiel 16, 23 and Hosea 1–3, is a commonplace in prophetic literature. The Book of Judges faults Israel's repeated, uncontrollable backsliding into idolatry. And the Deuteronomic history accuses most of the kings of both Israel and Judah of compromising with or favoring the worship of gods that, by Friedman's reckoning, had long since been declared dead, as in Elijah's devastating public humiliation (and mass slaughter) of the prophets of Baal in 1 Kings 18.

The most outrageous instance of the hold that foreign gods still had over the Jews would likely be Ezekiel's bizarre vision of the seventy elders of the House of Israel burning incense to every imaginable idol ... in the Temple itself (Ez. 8:7–16). This looks like an irate poetic fantasy rather than a real-life event; but the scene must have had some kind of objective correlative (the text purportedly dates to 593 BCE). Judah's religious leaders, end especially the idealized figure of King Josiah (640–609 BCE) and his associates, may have clung to the one God and Lord; but many of their compatriots obviously hedged their bets.

But for Friedman the supreme achievement of the Levites was the linkage of monotheism with a grand ethical system, culminating in the principle of loving one's neighbor as oneself (Lev. 19:18), with "neighbor" taken in the universal sense of fellow human. Is this just a rewording, or a splendid ratcheting up, of the Golden Rule, which is found in every major religious tradition, though often stated negatively, as in Rabbi Hillel's "Whatever is hateful to you, don't do to your neighbor" (Shabbat 31a)? In any case, this noble ideal looks to Friedman like a logical offshoot of the Levites' experience as precarious strangers/sojourners.

Though he wears his theology lightly and concentrates on textual interpretation, what Friedman offers is by implication a grand ecumenical, rather than a primarily historical, case. He sums up his position as follows: Monotheists are not necessarily superior to others morally. But monotheism and ethical treatment of all humans, whether they are members of the group or not, were both by-products of a common historical development. And that historical development was the Exodus. It did not have two million people who experienced it. But millions of us have been its heirs. That feeling is foreshadowed near the beginning of the Bible's story. Abraham's seed is to act in a way that will bring blessing to all earth's families. Can we not all take on the role of Abraham's seed? Not just Jews. Not just Christians. Not just Muslims.

Perhaps a bit of special pleading here (what about the Flood? the ethnic cleansing of Joshua? the savage —and non-mythic—punishments predicted by Moses in Deuteronomy 28?), but effective pleading nonetheless. Friedman thinks big and marshals an impressive array of clues. Unlike mundane detective stories, this one can't be definitively wrapped up and stored away. But it captures your attention.

*—Peter Heinegg*

## DO THEY CONTRADICT THEMSELVES? VERY WELL THEN THEY CONTRADICT THEMSELVES

*The People and the Books: 18 Classics of Jewish Literature.* By Adam Kirsch, New York: W.W. Norton, 2016. xxii + 407 pp. $28.95.

Adam Kirsch is a poet, critic, journalist, and director of the M.A. program in Jewish Studies at Columbia University. The task he undertakes here—a comprehensive survey of Jewish writing from the Bible to the twentieth century—is clearly impossible, especially since he's aiming at readers unfamiliar or marginally familiar with this mountain of material. And what polymathic prodigy could do full justice to all these diverse texts? No matter: despite some rough edges, Kirsch's fly-over reveals many expansive vistas that are well worth the trip.

Of course, the choice of readings is bound to be problematic. Kirsch comments on excerpts from eighteen sources (not coincidentally, in gematria 18 = "life"): Deuteronomy, the Book of Esther, Philo of Alexandria's *Exposition of the Law*, Josephus' *Jewish War*, the Talmudic tractate *Chapters of the Fathers*, Benjamin of Tudela's *Itinerary* and Yehuda Halevi's *Kuzari*, Maimonides' *Guide of the Perplexed*, the *Zohar*, the *Tsenerene* and the *Memoirs* of Glückel of Hameln, Spinoza's *Theological-Political Treatise*, the *Autobiography* of Solomon Maimon and Moses Mendelssohn's *Jerusalem*, the *Tales* of Nachman of Bratslav, Theodor Herzl's *Jewish State* and *Old New Land*, and finally Sholem Aleichem's *Tevye the Dairyman*.

Whew. But no prophets, major or minor? No Job or Psalms? No Joseph Caro? No Moses Luzzatto? No Heine, Peretz, Kafka, or Buber? (Qoheleth answered this objection in advance, when he said (12.12), "Of making many books there is no end.") Kirsch's treasure trove naturally defies summary, although he maintains it can be reduced to four basic themes: God, the Torah, the Land of Israel, and the Jewish people—a sound, if predictable, set of guidelines. But what the newcomer might find more surprising-provocative is the almost unrelenting contradictoriness of the authors, who are constantly at odds with their heritage, with one another, and sometimes with themselves. Judaism may have a recognizable central vision (or visions); but it has no party line; and a lively dissonance, rather than tame harmony, is its signature.

The trouble, or beauty of it all, begins in Deuteronomy (Greek for "second law" or "repetition of the law"). The text, or key parts of it, seems to be the "scroll" discovered by the high priest Hilkiah in the Temple during the reign of Josiah (622 BCE). The king is horrified because it reveals a body of law that the nation had been violating for centuries, in particular the foundational ban on idolatry. So forgetful had

Israel, now reduced to the southern kingdom of Judah, become that it no longer even kept the Passover. How could this catastrophic state of oblivion have come about, since Moses had thundered so forcefully (e.g., in Dt. 13) against worshiping false gods and delivered such precise directions for celebrating the Passover (in Ex. 12—even before the event had occurred)?

No explanation is given for this; but Kirsch calls Josiah's astonished encounter with the Torah the beginning of Jewish history. If so, it was a rather dark beginning; because the ferocious campaign the king subsequently led against Canaanite religion, destroying pagan shrines (the "high places") and butchering their priests, proved to be of no long-term avail. A generation after Josiah's death (609 BCE) the Babylonians sacked Jerusalem (586 BCE) and took the "cream" of the population off to exile in Babylon. Righteous as he was, Josiah's good deeds weighed less in the Lord's scale than the horrific crimes of his grandfather Manasseh (697–642 BCE), which included child sacrifice, and which ultimately doomed the country to its downfall (whence the perpetually nagging issue of corporate guilt). In one final insult, Josiah himself had been assured by the prophetess Huldah (2 Kings 22.20) that he would be "gathered to his grave in peace." But in fact Josiah was slain in battle at Megiddo by the Pharaoh Neco.

Back to Deuteronomy. In his last sermons to the Israelites supposedly gathered in the fields of Moab, Moses issues a vehement warning about what would later be called the Deuteronomic Principle: following the Law guarantees prosperity, breaking it brings disaster. The efficacy of this core rule could already be seen in the traumatic twist that the entire generation originally taking part in the Exodus, with the exception of Joshua and Caleb, perished in the wilderness and never entered the Promised Land—because of their idolatry, ingratitude, and refusal to trust the Lord. This was the same pattern of gross betrayal and radical failure than annihilated the Northern Kingdom of Israel in 722 BCE, when it fell to Assyria.

Moses winds up his discourse by conducting a choral recital of blessings and curses that will await the nation, depending on its fidelity or infidelity to the covenant. But the catalog of curses is much longer and more formidable; and it culminates in the grisly, hair-raising prediction of a future siege, unnamed but apparently pointing to the capture of Jerusalem by Nebuchadnezzar. Jeremiah 12 and Job 21 protest that the flourishing of the wicked belies the Deuteronomic Principle; but God won't explain why this is so; and, short of affirming a final judgment in the afterlife (essentially absent from the Tanakh), it's hard to see that the Principle is regularly enforced. And then Moses himself, after bearing forty years of bickering and enmity from his rebellious horde, is barred from crossing over into Canaan for the trivial reason (Num. 20.12) that he'd struck a rock to provide water for the Israelites when he was supposed to have merely ordered the rock to gush. Was this fair? Was this why Maimonides wrote that the good life was not a reward for obeying God, but a present to enable the Jews to "follow more commandments"? In any case, Kirsch stresses the stern vision of social justice laid out in Deuteronomy, which re-echoed in the New Testament and the Qur'an, and which may in the end have to be its own reward. But the jarring contrast remains between the bulk of the Book, which shows the road to the good life, and Moses' words, which mostly bemoan the people's stubborn incapacity to take it.

The only other book of the Bible Kirsch highlights is the late (perhaps as late as the Maccabean period) Book of Esther in a chapter entitled "In the Kingdom of Chance." It's only by chance that Mordecai learns about Haman's plans to wipe out all the Persian Jews. It's only by chance that Ahasuerus' (Xerxes') favorite wife manages to turn him against Haman, save the Jews, and then exterminate their enemies. God is nowhere mentioned in Esther (though the same is true of the Song of Solomon). The Jews, a word that recurs with startling frequency here, are an endangered minority. They are culturally assimilated: (Mordecai = Marduk, Esther =Ishtar) and have little connection to Israel except that Haman is an Agagite, a bloodthirsty descendant of evil Amalek, and Mordecai is a Benjaminite, like King Saul, in whose presence Samuel hacked Agag, king of the Amalekites, to pieces (1 Sam. 15.33).

Haman, now taken to be the quintessential model of Jew-haters, from the Pharaoh who didn't know Joseph to Hitler (and beyond), is defeated, not by divine providence and intervention, but by timely, lucky, aggressive self-defense.

The non-historical legend of Esther thus speaks to the "paradox of Jewish power in a condition of Diaspora": Insofar as they are weak, the Jews are natural targets of their foes. Insofar as a powerful individual Jew (cf. Mordecai's ultimate position as prime minister) protects his people, Jewish solidarity can be hostilely equated to Jewish difference, which was the rationale for Haman's planned genocide. But in both Israel and the modern western Galut today that danger appears to have largely dissipated.

In Philo of Alexandria (ca. 15 BCE–45 CE), we come up against another aspect of acculturation: the role of a scientifically and philosophically educated, Greek-speaking (and probably Hebrew-less) Jew in a multicultural city that is part of a multicultural empire. Philo allegorizes (since, as Paul would say, "the letter killeth") and meditates about Scripture in a way that is "religious," but seems entirely removed from the spirit and flavor of the original. For instance, in discussing the account(s) of creation in Genesis, Philo says that the main purpose of the heavenly bodies that light up the darkness is to get humans (those of a thoughtful cast anyway) to meditate on "the substance of these things which are visible... and what the causes are by which everything is regulated." In the first, "Priestly" version, what God creates is the *idea* of humans. And there was no concrete Garden of Eden, with a tree of knowledge and a tree of life. The latter is just a symbol of piety, the greatest of the virtues, "by means of which the soul is made immortal." What Genesis teaches is (1) that God really exists, (2) that God is one, (3) that the world is not eternal, (4) that there is only one world, and (5) that God takes care of it. And when God chooses the little nation of Israel, it just means he prefers a small company of good individuals "to an infinite number of persons who are unjust." Philo has interpreted Jewish texts to make them compatible with a generic, abstract monotheism. But is this Judaism? In his chapter on Josephus (37-ca. 100 CE), ambiguously titled "Choosing Life," Kirsch follows another between-two-worlds aristocratic Jew.

Flavius Josephus, born Yosef ben Mattiyahu ha-Kohen, fought as a general on both sides of the Jewish War (66–70 CE) and stood with the triumphant Romans as the Temple of Jerusalem went up in flames. Josephus artfully endeared himself to Vespasian by predicting his rise to emperor and spent the last three decades of his life in Rome. He presents himself as a patriotic Jew (he was also, as his name indicates, a priest), who rejected the violent extremism of the Zealots and saw the Roman armies as a world-historical power that could not and should not be resisted. But he was always aware of the ambiguity of his position, and he treated the suicides at Masada as a grand and noble deed. He has the rebel leader Eleazar tell the warriors that their defeat was a punishment from God; and that since "life is the calamity for man, not death, which gives freedom to our souls," they must all welcome death. Josephus defended himself from charges of abandoning his people and of cowardice (i.e., for not joining any of the suicide missions his brethren went on). However much guilt he may have felt, Josephus opted for rational submission to the gentile powers that be (i.e., survival), while remaining true to Judaism.

Rather than venture out into the oceanic expanse of the Talmud, Kirsch sensibly limits himself to its best known section, the *Pirkei Avot* (Chapters of the Fathers), composed around 250 CE. He sees it as the crucial link between the destruction of the Temple in 70 CE and the spread of a new normative Jewish culture, led by rabbis and centered on the synagogue and the study of sacred texts in the *beit midrash*. All the elaborate rites of animal sacrifice could no longer be performed, and even before the collapse of the Bar Kochba revolt in 135 CE the majority of Jews lived outside Israel. And so a dreadful disaster gave birth to a fruitful alternative tradition.

Understandably, Kirsch stresses the wisdom and moral power of the great sages in *Avot:* Yochanan ben Zakkai, Akiva, Hillel, Tarfon, etc.; and he delights in citing them. But he also notes somewhat casually the darker aspects of rabbinical wisdom: misogyny

("When a man talks too much to his wife, he causes evil to himself, disregards the words of the Torah, and in the end will inherit Gehinnom [Hell]"); contempt for the physical world ("The more flesh, the more worms; the more possessions, the more worry; the more wives, the more witchcraft; the more maidservants, the more lewdness; the more menservants, the more theft"); and a kind of fanatical, elitist intellectualism ("One who does not study deserves to die"). Were these all side-effects of strong medicine? Were they avoidable?

The Talmud replaced the Temple and was an infinitely more impressive achievement (besides, the very notion of a temple was foreign, derived from Egypt and Mesopotamia). It bound, and still binds, the Jewish world together, even after the emergence of the state of Israel. And the fierce intellectual dedication that created and grew out of it helped launch the amazing creativity of secular Jewish thinkers, artists, scientists, etc. in the wake of the Haskalah.

In "The Scandal of Chosenness" Kirsch deals briefly with Benjamin of Tudela (1130–1173), whose *Itinerary* spanned the Jewish world from Spain to Iran, at once taking pride in the far-flung communities of his fellow Jews and bemoaning their oppression in Palestine under the Crusaders. More importantly, he discusses Yehudah Halevi (ca. 1075–1141), another Spaniard, a physician and poet, whose *Kuzari*, a Platonic dialogue between a rabbi and the king of the Khazars, a Turkish tribe that converted to Judaism in the eighth century, prizes revelation over philosophy and celebrates the superiority of the Jews and their faith. "The law was given to us," the rabbi insists, "because He led us out of Egypt, and remained attached to us, because we are the pick of mankind."

The chosenness of the Jews has always scandalized Gentiles (although Christians and Muslims have their own varieties of it); but the rabbi makes no bones about Jewish exceptionalism. He informs the king that even after conversion the Khazars won't enjoy complete equality with the Jews. The rabbi —and Kirsch—might have added that the Bible often presents the state of election as burdensome, if not terrifying, as in Amos 3.2: "You only have I known of all the families of the earth; *therefore* I will punish you for all your iniquities." God never tells Abraham why he and his descendants were chosen. And Moses emphasizes (Dt. 9.4-5) that God was not granting the Israelites a home in Canaan because of their righteousness or integrity, but because of the wickedness of the original inhabitants.

If at all possible, the rabbi continues, Jews should try to reach the Holy Land, even if they die in the effort, as the rabbi assumes that he will, and as Halevi himself did (though the dramatic account of his being killed by an Arab horseman at the gates of Jerusalem seems to be mythical). "The holiness of the Land becomes a corollary of the holiness of the Jewish people. To believe in either, the rabbi argues, is to defy reason and to trust in the authority of prophecy, tradition, and miracle."

Halevi stands in sharp contrast with Moses Maimonides (1135–1204), whose *Guide of the Perplexed*, an attempt to harmonize the Bible and Aristotle, may go down as one of the noblest lost causes in theological history. Maimonides severely demythologizes Scripture, rejecting *all* anthropomorphic language about God (making humans in his image, walking in the Garden of Eden, becoming enraged or changing his mind). Aside from not having a body, God has no needs and desires, which raises the age-old question: Why, if he is so perfectly transcendent, should God care about humans and their doings? Maimonides denies Aristotle's belief in the eternity of the universe; but then something must have caused the Unmoved Mover to create it and to take part in human affairs. Angels are natural forces, not winged messengers. Prophecy is a kind of mental perfection, and there is a rational basis for every one of the *mitzvot* (circumcision serves to lessen unruly male lust; and many laws, like the ban on mixing different fabrics, are designed to thwart idolatry), and so forth. Despite the veneration accorded Maimonides (although he was also criticized, e.g., for his lukewarm affirmation of life after death), his assertion that the intellect, not moral behavior, shapes the relationship of the individual to God seems not to jibe with the Torah's unrelenting emphasis on obedience. As with some other members of Kirsch's pantheon, one wonders how much Maimonides' thinking affected the mind and heart of ordinary Jews, especially since he framed the *Guide* in arcane, if not obscure language so as to limit his audience to Jewish cognoscenti.

The most baffling work (some 2,400 pages long) that Kirsch focuses on is the *Zohar*, mostly composed, it appears, by the Spanish Kabbalist Moses de Leon (ca. 1240–1305), though it purports to date back to the second century CE. Described by Gershom Scholem (the world's greatest expert on the subject) as a "mystical novel" and the virtual antithesis of the teaching of Maimonides, the *Zohar* (Heb. Splendor) envisions a kind of erotic connection between the unknowable, infinite God (*En Sof*), and human beings. Through a series of emanations (*sefirot*), God passes down to his ultimate manifestation, the *Shekhinah* (= a feminized divine presence, which also symbolizes the Assembly of Israel). When the emanation known as *Tiferet* (Beauty) and *Malkhut* (Kingdom) are linked in marital bliss, the world is blessed. But when they are disjoined, trouble ensues. Human action plays a key role in this: good deeds promote union, sins bring about chaos. "Judaism," Kirsch summarizes, "is not just an arbitrary set of commandments and prohibitions, but a technology for bringing God into harmony with himself. The *Zohar* brought to Judaism something that the austere philosophy of the Middle Ages lacked: the sense that God needs man as much as man needs God."

Kirsch's chapter, "Daughters of Zion," on the *Tsenerene* and the *Memoirs* of Glückel of Hameln (1646–1724) is a welcome, low-key interval after all the preceding complexities. On the other hand, Glückel's is the sole woman's voice in the volume, so we're reminded that Judaism is as male-dominated as most other religious traditions. The *Tsenerene* ("Come and See," from the Song of Songs. 3.11) first published in the 1590s, was a Yiddish devotional work, aimed at women but written by a man, Joseph ben Isaac Ashkenazi, and popular with men as well, that offered moral lessons and fanciful *midrashim*. "Our Sages say that during Sarah's lifetime her candles burned from one Shabbat eve to another; the dough she kneaded was blessed; and a cloud hovered over her tent." It contains faint hints of feminism, as in its commentary on Adam's telling God that he ate the forbidden fruit because Eve had given it to him: "What kind of answer is that? If his wife had given it to him, did that make him guiltless? Was Adam so stupid that he listened to his wife after God had forbidden him to eat?" But for the most part, the *Tsenerene* simply preaches conventional piety and wifely modesty.

Glückel of Hameln, the author of the first Jewish female autobiography, was a German businesswoman and mother, a shrewd, energetic, uncomplicatedly orthodox woman. Having to overcome the financial incompetence of various male family members who died or left her in the lurch, Glückel displays a gritty energy and toughness. She conveys a vivid sense of what life was like in a world where Jews might occasionally prosper, but were still marginalized and persecuted. It's a shame that not more of her sisters (and brothers) wrote down their experiences in her own and earlier times.

There was no way Kirsch could have omitted Spinoza, and he wrestles with him mightily in "Heresy and Freedom," which addresses the *Theological-Political Treatise* (1670). Much has always been made (and rightly so) of Spinoza's brutal excommunication by the Jewish community of Amsterdam on July 27, 1656 (see the fine Yiddish poem *Der Herem* by Melech Ravitch) most nineteenth and twentieth century Yiddish writers were apostates and often identified with the outcast genius). Spinoza's equation of God with Nature was, effectively, atheism, however pervaded by a pantheistic mystique; and his *Treatise*, which pleads in his unmistakable calm, clear, unemotional style for freedom of speech and the necessity of reading the Bible as an utterly fallible, time-bound piece of literature, paved the way for secular biblical scholarship.

For Spinoza, there can be no miracles, because nothing can happen in violation of the laws of nature (as Hume would later profess). Prophets thought they were seeing visions; but they were just highly imaginative persons. Biblical ethics boils down to this: "There exists a supreme being who loves justice and charity, and that, to be saved, all people must obey and venerate Him by practicing justice and charity towards their neighbor." (Except that "He" is not a person, only the eternal, unchanging order of the universe.) One might speculate that Spinoza's thinking was, in part anyhow, rooted in the frequent blasts of prophets like Amos, Isaiah, Jeremiah, et al., who excoriated people for fussing over empty rituals while neglecting to do the right thing. The chosenness of the Jews was childish vanity.

Spinoza, then, is an Anti-Judaic Jew (he mastered Hebrew and never converted). Daniel B. Schwartz (George Washington University) calls him "the first modern Jew," whence his place in Jewish history as the forerunner of hundreds of thousands of non-religious Jews, who consciously or unconsciously embrace Spinoza's ideals, but cling to one or other version of *Yiddishkeit*. The list of great Jewish heretics is a staggeringly long one.

In "Between Two Worlds," Kirsch follows the rocky road of the Jewish Enlightenment in eighteenth century Germany, as seen in the *Autobiography* of Solomon Maimon (1753–1800) and *Jerusalem* by Moses Mendelssohn (1729–1786). Maimon, born Shlomo ben Yehoshua in a Lithuanian *shtetl*, and Mendelssohn, born Moshe ben Mendel in the city of Dessau, were both Talmudic *Wunderkinder* who ventured into semi-welcoming intellectual circles of the *Aufklärer*. Maimon, who was desperately poor and uncouth, mostly crashed. A lonely autodidact, he wandered through Germany and Holland, and barely kept body and soul together by teaching classical Jewish texts he no longer believed in, and composing recondite Hebrew monographs on metaphysics and theology. His model and mentor was the highly successful Moses Mendelssohn, who was immortalized in Lessing's *Nathan the Wise* (1779).

Mendelssohn wanted to build a bridge between authentic, but rationalized Judaism and European culture. In *Jerusalem* (1783), he called for freedom of religion and the separation of church and state. He downplayed doctrine, noting that, "Among all the prescriptions and ordinances of the Mosaic Law, there is not a single one which says: *"You shall believe or not believe."* Judaism had by and large done without creeds, with even Maimonides' "Thirteen Principles of Faith" winning only modest acceptance. Jews were to be good citizens by obeying both the laws of the country they found themselves in and Jewish law, even though they were under no constraint to do the latter.

Immanuel Kant thought *Jerusalem* "irrefutable," but much of German Jewry went off on paths Mendelssohn would have, to say the least, disapproved: conversion to Christianity, usually Protestantism, adherence to the Reform movement, or downright godlessness (Karl Marx and company). Four of his own children converted; and his grandson, Felix, became a devoutly Lutheran composer.

Kirsch deals with the vast topic of Hasidism somewhat quixotically by talking not so much about its founder, the Baal Shem Tov (ca. 1700–1760) but the eccentric storyteller Nachman of Bratslav (1772–1810). This is in keeping with his literary bias, but it passes over the shape of life in Hassidic communities. Unfortunately, just recounting the ingenious twisted plots of a handful of Nachman's celebrated Tales doesn't get us very far. One thing they do make plain is the exalted figure of the *tzaddik*. But, as readers of I.B. Singer know, this could often lead to cult-like aberrations (see the rebbe's "court" or the custom of devoutly eating *shiyadim*, the leftovers from his plate), from arrogant domineering to downright craziness. *Tzaddikim* were often credited with working miraculous cures and other preternatural feats. In fairness to the *mitnagdim* (the traditionalist opponents of the Hassidim), one would have liked to hear something about this.

Kirsch's penultimate chapter, "If You Will It," treats the sublimely ironic figure of Theodor Herzl (1860–1904), the mediocre playwright and completely assimilated Jew, ignorant of his own religion, who turned the Diaspora upside down. Surveying *The Jewish State* and his utopian novel *Old New Land*, Kirsch observes that Herzl held the millennial Jewish longing for Zion at arm's length. He saw the resurrected homeland as a multicultural, polyglot, technologically advanced western-style socialist republic. He got almost all the details about the future state of Israel wrong: Emigration would take twenty years, in one enormous wave, financed by an elaborate investment scheme (among other things, two million pounds of tribute would have to be paid to the Turks). There would no serious resistance from the Arabs; the country would bloom with picturesque, German-named little villages. The national flag would be a white field with seven golden stars to represent, believe it or not, the progressive seven-hour work day. Nothing of this came true; but with its visionary power and perfect timing (in the wake of the Dreyfus case and the murderous rising tide of anti-Semitism), *The Jewish State* launched an astonishing revolution that is still defining itself.

The final text Kirsch offers is *Tevye the Dairyman* by Sholem Aleichem, who could no more have imagined the transformation of his stories into a sensational Broadway musical hit than Herzl could have imagined the rise and runaway spread of the *Haredim* in contemporary Israel. This is an apt choice since *Tevye* features a wise, warm, practical-minded man (with a rich, if haphazard Jewish education) facing in his own life and the lives of his daughters the massive challenges and seductions of modernity, including individualism, political turmoil, intermarriage, and ever more brutal Jew-hatred. Most grimly, the setting of Tevye's adventures is in and around the city he called Yehupetz—Kiev, where on September 29 and 30, 1941 the Germans murdered the entire Jewish population in the ravine of Babi Yar. Tevye's *landsleit* could cope with tsarist pogroms, but not Nazi *Einsatzgruppen*.

"The Tevye stories," Kirsch claims, "carry us to the very brink of the Jewish world we inhabit today." A century after the death of Sholem Aleichem in 1916 (in New York!) that world evidently contains such an enormous, bewildering host of texts, orthodox, secular, and in-between, that go back to one or more of Kirsch's eighteen, but that can't be readily classified or synthesized. And right from the start, there was no way to escape a certain arbitrariness in his canon.

His selections provide a bird's eye view of a territory that would require, and has taken up, many lifetimes to properly explore. Above all they offer striking proof of an incorrigibly restless spirit, of minds unwilling to stay within the boundaries of what they were raised with—or to leave them completely behind. "I am nothing if not critical," Iago sneered. But what Kirsch introduces the reader to here exemplifies critical thinking at its finest, at once passionate and detached, fearless and rational, broad and specific, proud and generous. In a quirky touch Kirsch never cites chapter and verse for his countless quotations. Perhaps he was trying to reduce the apparatus to an absolute minimum: There are no footnotes either, and only the skimpiest of bibliographies. Professors teaching this otherwise accessible and helpful book will find that an irritant. But, since it's only a preliminary guide, perhaps Kirsch wanted to send his readers off to dig into the sources on their own. They have, in any case, a demanding and rewarding long haul ahead of them.

—*Peter Heinegg*

# CONTRIBUTORS

**Philip R. Corlett** is Assistant Professor of Psychiatry at the Yale School of Medicine. He trained in Experimental Psychology, Cognitive Neuroscience and Psychiatry at the University of Cambridge, won a Wellcome Trust Prize Studentship, and completed his Ph.D. on the brain bases of delusion formation in the Brain Mapping Unit, Department of Psychiatry. After a short postdoc, he was awarded the University of Cambridge Parke-Davis Exchange Fellowship in Biomedical Sciences which brought him to the Yale University Department of Psychiatry to explore the maintenance of delusions. He was named a Rising Star and Future Opinion Leader by Pharmaceutical Marketing Magazine and joined the Yale faculty in 2011. He currently explores the cognitive and biological mechanisms of delusional beliefs as well as predictive learning, habit formation, and addiction at the Belief, Learning and Memory Lab (BLAM). He is also a member of the Yale Interdepartmental Neuroscience Program. For more information, visit

http://psychiatry.yale.edu/people/philip_corlett.profile

**Brett J. Esaki** is Assistant Professor in Department of Religious Studies at Georgia State University and the director of Graduate Studies. His most recent book, "Enfolding Silence: The Transformation of Japanese American Religion and Art under Oppression," was published by Oxford University Press as part of their AAR Academy Series in 2016.

**Anne Foerst** is Associate Professor of Computer Science at St. Bonaventure University and the director of SBU's Individualized Major program. She is also directing SBU's Certiport Microsoft Office Licensing program. For her postdoctoral research, she joined the MIT Artificial Intelligence in 1995 as theological adviser to the two social robot projects Cog and Kismet and then joined the SBU faculty in 2001. She has spoken and published widely in the area of theology and robots, ecclesiology and the Internet, and the Biblical, religious, and psychological construct of personhood. For more information, see

http://www.cs.sbu.edu/afoerst/

**Benjamin Gross** is Assistant Professor for Sociology at St. Bonaventure University. He holds a Ph.D. in Sociology from Michigan State University (2010) and has since then taught at SBU. His research focuses on political sociology, especially in its online forms, and on the interaction of media, particularly social media, and society. For more information, visit

http://www.sbu.edu/about-sbu/people-of-sbu/faculty-profiles/gross-benjamin

**Peter Heinegg** was born in Brooklyn, spent seven years in Jesuit seminaries, received a B.A. in English from Fordham University, and received a Ph.D. in Comparative Literature from Harvard University. He has taught at Harvard, Queens College, C.U.N.Y, and at Union College in Schenectady, where he is a professor of English and Comparative

Literature. He is the author of numerous translations of books on religion and theology, of book reviews, and volumes of collected essays on religion and contemporary culture. He has contributed to the Christianity section of the Norton Anthology of World Religion. His special interests include the Bible, anti-Semitism, and the history of belief and unbelief in 19th century Europe.

peterheinegg@hotmail.com

**Tobi Kahn** is a painter and sculptor whose work has been shown in over 40 solo exhibitions and over 60 museum and groups shows since he was selected as one of nine artists to be included in the 1985 Guggenheim Museum exhibition, New Horizons, in American Art. Works by Kahn are in major museum, corporate, and private collections. For thirty years, Kahn has been steadfast in the pursuit of his distinct vision and persistent in his commitment to the redemptive possibilities of art. In paint, stone, and bronze, he has explored the correspondence between the intimate and monumental. While his early works drew on the tradition of American Romantic landscape painting, his more recent pieces reflect his fascination with contemporary science, inspired by the microimages of cell formations and satellite photography For twenty-five years, Kahn has been making miniature sacred spaces he calls "shrines." The first full-scale shrine, Shalev, is in New Harmony, Indiana, commissioned as an outdoor sculpture for Jane Owen and the Robert Lee Blaffer Trust.

**Manfred Oeming** is Professor of Old Testament Theology and the University of Heidelberg, Germany. In the forefront of Prof. Oeming's research and teaching are the themes of historiography in Israel, the Psalms, Biblical archeology, and the Jewish–Christian dialogue. He is vice president of the College for Jewish Studies (Heidelberg) and has been active as a visiting professor in Jerusalem. Included in his publications are the monographs "Gesamtbiblische Theologie der Gegenwart. Das Verhältnis von AT und NT," "Das wahre Israel. Die genealogische Vorhalle 1 Chr 1-9," "Einführung in die Biblische Hermeneutik," and a commentary on the Psalms. Prof. Oeming has written numerous articles, among others for the lexicon RGG (fourth edition). For more information, visit

http://www.uni-heidelberg.de/fiit/personen/oeming_en.html

www.ingramcontent.com/pod-product-compliance
Lightning Source LLC
Chambersburg PA
CBHW040300170426
**43193CB00020B/2963**